. . . were carried by the electric railways of America. ↑Under a lowering Utah sky, the Bamberger Railroad's electric locomotive #551 transports coal and merchandise in freight cars of the Denver & Rio Grande Western Railroad, Southern Railway System, Pennsylvania Railroad and Utah Coal Route. FRED FELLOW, W. C. WHITTAKER COLLECTION

Not Only Passengers
How the Electric Railways Carried Freight, Express and Baggage
Bulletin 129 of the Central Electric Railfans' Association

Not Only Passengers

How the Electric Railways Carried Freight, Express and Baggage

Bulletin 129 of the
Central Electric Railfans' Association
Text: Roy G. Benedict and James R. McFarlane
Photographs: Many sources, credited where they appear
Project management: Norman Carlson
Other acknowledgments appear on pages 122–124

Library of Congress Catalog Card Number 92-71563
International Standard Book Number 0-915348-29-2

Published by Central Electric Railfans' Association, Post Office Box 503, Chicago, Illinois 60690-0503, United States of America

←*On page 1:* **Hershey Transit Company box motor #25 heads east toward Lebanon (Pa.) from Elizabethtown Junction on December 16, 1941.** H. L. GOLDSMITH

Introduction

Not Only Passengers is a study of freight transportation on the electric street and interurban railways in the United States and Canada. These trolleys, like today's mass transit, carried mainly short-haul passengers; but freight, express and baggage gave them another way to aid local commerce and bring in revenue. Built mainly in 1890–1910, they flourished for a time, but weakened by the growing availability of private road transport many expired during the Great Depression of the 1930's. However, as this book shows, a few continue in some form even today to carry "not only passengers."

Small, almost miniature, industrial electric railways for internal material handling existed within many mines, mills, coke works and factories. And at the opposite extreme were the electrified divisions of the general railroads, differing from other segments only by using electric power rather than steam locomotives to haul freight and passenger trains. Neither of these two extremes in electric railroading technology is the subject of *Not Only Passengers.*

Some railway freight terms, shown *in italics* where they first occur, are either explicitly defined or explained in context. Phonetic pronunciations are given (in parentheses) for place names which may not often be heard spoken outside their regions.

The coverage of this book is nationwide rather than local or regional. It is not a close study of the methods of any one railroad—such a treatment is best left to books about the individual carriers, and some of them have done it very well indeed.

In this book individual railways are mentioned as examples of practices also found elsewhere. An attempt was made to note cases in various regions. Different examples, and many more of them, could be found. We encourage readers to consider how similar situations were handled on the railways with which they are most familiar.

Indeed, *Not Only Passengers* is an opportunity for you, the reader, to enjoy thinking about how the street and interurban trolleys contributed to the economy of their time by carrying "not only passengers."

Contents

←Passengers on electric lines bring belongings; thus cars for interurban service have baggage racks. On the South Shore Line, train 25 of March 7, 1983 departs from Gary (Ind.) carrying "not only passengers." DONALD R. KAPLAN, SHORE LINE INTERURBAN HISTORICAL SOCIETY COLLECTION

Most electric railways were planned to carry passengers, not freight. Often cities flatly ruled out hauling freight on street trackage—almost all electric railways involved street running.

Even so, right from the first day of operation, the railways carried more than just passengers. The passengers naturally brought along their belongings. If it rained, the streetcars and interurbans carried passengers with umbrellas. On a fine holiday—passengers with "fish poles, lunch baskets and other picnic paraphernalia." In the commercial districts—"drummers" (salesmen) with their sample trunks. To the courthouse—lawyers with briefcases. To the railroad station—travelers with luggage. Truly the story of electric railways has always been a story of "not only passengers."

Airline passengers today are familiar with *carry-on luggage*. It's limited and regulated.

On the rails, the same concept was called *hand baggage* and it was not so closely regulated. But in either case, it consisted of things which the passengers brought with them and tended themselves, not material entrusted to the transportation company to deliver.

The company was involved nevertheless. One day a physician forgot his demonstration skeleton on a car! If bank employees were robbed while carrying a bag of money to a branch bank (when a thousand dollars was a thousand dollars) the streetcar company got some unwanted attention. Before nationwide prohibition in 1919, men carrying heavy suitcases of bottled goods made up part of the riding into "dry" counties. An occasional raid on a train by enforcement agents was an annoyance to the crew—and a bigger annoyance to the former owners of those suitcases!

City streetcars had no specific place for hand baggage. The streetcars were everyman's

Chapter 1 You

Riders brought baggage aboard, so electric railway cars carried "not only passengers."

transportation, so they accommodated everyone's possessions. It was always a problem to draw the line what could be brought onto the cars—perhaps not "trunks, chests, lumber, large packages, explosive materials, baby carriages . . . or articles which from their odor or otherwise, would be offensive to passengers." Animals were out of the question except for small pet dogs. Before folding strollers, baby buggies were a special problem. A few cities let mothers hang the carriages on special hooks outside the rear dash of the cars. Some companies tried to keep packages in an out-of-the-way location such as the front platform. One car line brought freshly caught fish to town strung across the front dash of the cars!

Such rules seldom worked out. People don't like to be separated from their belongings! If the car was half-empty, bundles rested on an unoccupied seat. Wide aisles intended for easy circulation of short-distance passengers just as easily held the housewives' big wicker shopping baskets. Carpenters going to or from jobs stowed their heavy tool boxes under the seats. The big back platform of a Pay As You Enter car in two-man days had room for a coal passer with the badges of his occupation: a big shovel and general grime. The streetcar companies were glad to have your fare (when a nickel was a nickel). They received nothing extra for what you carried.

In interurban service, there was more hand baggage, and larger pieces, because passengers made long trips. The rural lines had to provide space in the cars. Parcel racks of wire mesh or ornate foundry work accommodated small luggage overhead, getting it off the floor or passengers' laps. Stowing parcels was a chore for women or older people but that was no problem (when gentlemen were gentlemen). Having

luggage up there left room for mischance. One reported bump on the head occurred because a rifle fell out of the rack during a minor derailment while the students of a military academy were traveling. An alternative, found in some cars in Pittsburgh and elsewhere, was to provide parcel shelves in one corner of the car. This plan meant a 2% loss in seating capacity, perhaps a poor idea on busy lines. The open cars on the isolated Alpine Division of the Pacific Electric Railway were equipped with folding luggage shelves outboard of the dash.

If you were nervous about your baggage, you could buy insurance from the ticket agent. The insurance company paid commissions to both the agent and the railway.

What is the situation today? Rapid transit lines make up most of the electric railway industry now. They always had business commuters with attaché cases and downtown shoppers with neatly wrapped bundles. Some lines which extend to major airports are attracting travellers with luggage and even uniformed flight crews, the latter with their flight bags on collapsible two-wheel carriers. Trials of assigned shelf or rack space for airport luggage seemingly have not yet found the right combination to get wide usage.

Since the 1970's, several light rail and rapid transit systems have allowed bicycles on trains outside of the busy hours. This service adds a recreational opportunity in a large metropolitan area. Bicycles are placed by the owners in designated open space or in wheelchair areas (all new transit vehicles in the United States must accommodate people in wheelchairs).

People with such obvious cargo are only a small part of total transit riding, but they show that today as in the past, the electric railway industry serves "not only passengers."

Can Take It with You

↑**At Hope (Ia.) trunks are checked on the Fort Dodge Line.** ALBERT PARKS BUTTS, ALLAN C. WILLIAMS COLLECTION

The steam railroads carried *checked baggage* so that the passenger need not give it any attention during the trip. It travelled in the baggage car, not with the riders. Of course *checked luggage* on airlines today is the same idea. To compete with the railroads, many interurban railways offered the same service and checked 150 pounds free. With the nicety found in railroad rates everywhere, that translated to 75 pounds on a child's half-fare ticket. The Twin City Rapid Transit Company transferred baggage at three docks from its baggage train to its own steamboats on Lake Minnetonka near Minneapolis. Electric lines that had interline ticketing with steam railroads often checked baggage through.

Individuals or business enterprises frequently send small parcels though they have no one travelling. Until 1913, the United States Mail had a limit of 4 pounds—no parcel post. Besides, speed of delivery is often important. The result was the *express* business. Both city and interurban railways ran a parcel business under various names such as *dispatch freight, fast package service* and *package express.*

Some city railways conducted express business in their own names. On others it was operated by affiliates or contractors such as the St. Louis Express Company or the Merchants Express Company. Also at St. Louis, the United Railways Company leased an express motor to the Lewis Publishing Company. It received bags of *Woman's Magazine* and *Woman's Farm Journal* from wagons or battery-powered electric trucks and carried them to the post office.

A city line might not even have a freight station, but just park its express car for an hour each day on a dead track downtown and do business right on the car. Small enclosed cars were used, the size and outline of a city passenger streetcar of the same era but with few windows. A few cities, however, had roofed flat cars with end cabs. They probably never went fast enough to bounce the cargo off the open sides! With this service, city merchants could send supplies such as butcher orders or crates of eggs to outlying households. The merchants could buy package stamps from the railway and put the cost on customers' accounts. A modern innovation, the telephone, provided a convenient way to order goods.

The Norfolk (Va.) & Atlantic Terminal Company enjoyed rush business on Tuesdays, Thursdays and Saturdays from a market in its terminal building. Car crews brought people's shopping lists into town. Like Norfolk, the railways might as well formalize this traffic and get some revenue out of it, or people would find obliging carmen to do quick shopping in town for them. A gift of a cake to a regular motorman made him adept at carrying products from a bakery to storekeepers along the car line when the roads were bad in wet weather.

On the outskirts of some cities, car lines with infrequent service would leave a freight trailer on the main track. It was up to the consignees to unload it in time for the next passenger car to push it back to town!

Interurban lines did their express business, at least the most time-sensitive parts of it, on

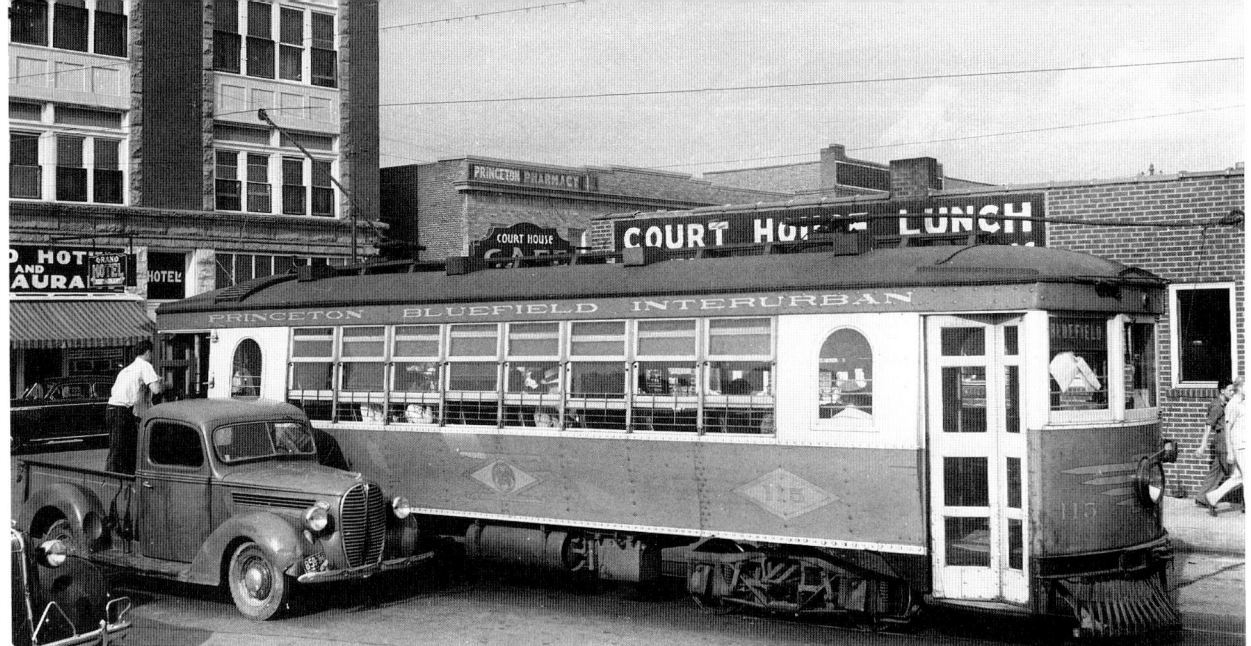

↑Lightweights like this Cincinnati Car Company product carried baggage and express too. Tri-City Traction Company #115 loads in Princeton (W. Va.) for a 12-mile run to Bluefield in the south part of the state. WILLIAM C. JANSSEN

the hourly passenger cars. With the frequent headway, specialized printers in small cities could compete with plants in the metropolis. Cut flowers went to local florists in Ontario towns on the Lake Erie & Northern Railway. Laboratories received white mice in crates, eggs went to fish hatcheries, and live baby chicks were distributed throughout raising regions. Beer in kegs or cases and ice cream in wooden tubs went to outlying retailers, and the empty containers came back. Repair parts for farm implements travelled by interurban. A box of ball bearings was small but heavy. Remains could be shipped by express, accompanied by an honor guard if military remains. On the British Columbia Electric Railway, daffodil bulbs were sent by express from Bradner (B. C.) even after electric passenger service ended in 1950. The last interurban express, lasting until about 1973, was the *emergency package service* of the Chicago South Shore & South Bend Railroad.

Merchandise was transloaded to and from boats on rivers, the Great Lakes and elsewhere, even ocean ships at San Diego. In the early 1960's the North Shore Line carried shipments in connection with Emery Air Freight.

In some regions, connecting interurban railways formed an *express company* to operate over those lines. The Electric Package Agency (originally Electric Package Company) at Cleveland (1898–1937) was especially long-lived. Unable to get traffic originating or terminating beyond the lines it served, such an agency was not a full solution to shippers' needs.

Express companies not related to the interurbans filled a wider need. They had a reputation for paying up if a shipment was lost. A shipper could take his parcel to the express agent or, in the cities, have a wagon call for it. Delivery was made in the same way. The shipper did not have to plan the routing or even know what railroads would participate. The express companies were quite willing to route via interurban for short hauls where the greater frequency overcame slower running times. Many an express shipment went by both steam and electric railroads with transfer at the junction city via express company wagon.

The railway was paid monthly for providing cars and stations and transporting the express shipments. In most towns, the interurban agent earned a 10% commission on the business originating or terminating at his station.

d Fifty Pounds Free

The express business had developed regionally since the 1830's. At the beginning of the interurban era there were several major "old line" express companies: Adams Express Company along the Eastern seaboard and in the South; American Express Company primarily in the Northeast and the Midwest; Southern Express on the Southern Railway System and smaller lines in the same general territory; United States Express Company (liquidated about 1915) mostly in Illinois, Indiana, Ohio and Michigan; and Wells Fargo & Company mainly in the West but also providing some service as far east as New York. Several smaller companies also existed, such as the National Express Company in New York and New England. Railways contracted with these express companies, generally only one of them at a time although it was common to change from one to another over the years. The side of interurban cars often displayed the herald of the express company. In 1910 Canadian intercity lines were home to the Canadian Express Company or Dominion Express Company, later to the Canadian National Express, Canadian Pacific Express Company or both.

In July 1918, the express business of the old-line companies was combined into American Railway Express, Inc., which covered the entire United States. The companies themselves continued financial services so that two of their names are still familiar in 1992. Unlike its predecessors, the unified company favored the railroads and avoided electric lines where it could. However, it contracted with a few of the larger interurban railways for as long as passenger service existed. In 1918–1938, it had regional competition in the form of Southeastern Express Company, which operated over some railroads and interurbans. In March 1929, American Railway Express became Railway Express Agency, Inc. and in 1970 REA Express, Inc. (formalizing a trade name in use for ten years) but by then even the railroads, let alone interurbans, were practically irrelevant to it. REA was liquidated in the late 1970's.

Checked baggage outlasted express companies. Indeed, baggage can be checked today (1992) on principal Amtrak trains, hardly interurban service even where electrified.

Combines

In the small interurban trains, one car or a few cars, baggage or express had no car to itself, nor was checked baggage separated from express. In many parts of the country the typical interurban car had a space about 8 feet square in one end fitted as a baggage room. A few early New England properties even achieved this in a single-truck car.

At town stations the agent or helper wheeled the station baggage cart alongside the car. Wide sliding side doors eased loading of large luggage. This exchange took place every hour or so right in the middle of Main Street! Of course, today's level of auto traffic did not exist then.

In single-end cars the baggage compartment, in two-man days, was at the front of the car. The motorman could unload shipments for the country stops or help the town agents with heavy pieces. Unlike the railroads, few interurbans had enough traffic on any one train to need a baggageman or messenger of the express company aboard. The motorman received no extra pay for handling the cargo—it was just part of the job if he chose to work for an interurban line.

In theory tending express while the train was standing at stations fit in well with running the train from one point to another. In practice it was sometimes different. After a fatal head-on collision, investigators reported that motormen frequently recorded express shipments on waybills while running trains "especially when the consignment is heavy or the train is late"! In this case, the car heating stoves upset and ignited nitrate movie films and newspapers which made up much of the load, so that three wooden passenger cars were completely burned.

Folding wooden seats in the baggage compartment accommodated the overflow crowds on Sundays and county fair days. Sometimes this space also served as the smoking compartment although there was a trend, in later interurban cars, to have a third compartment as a smoker. On many lines, you rode with the baggage if you

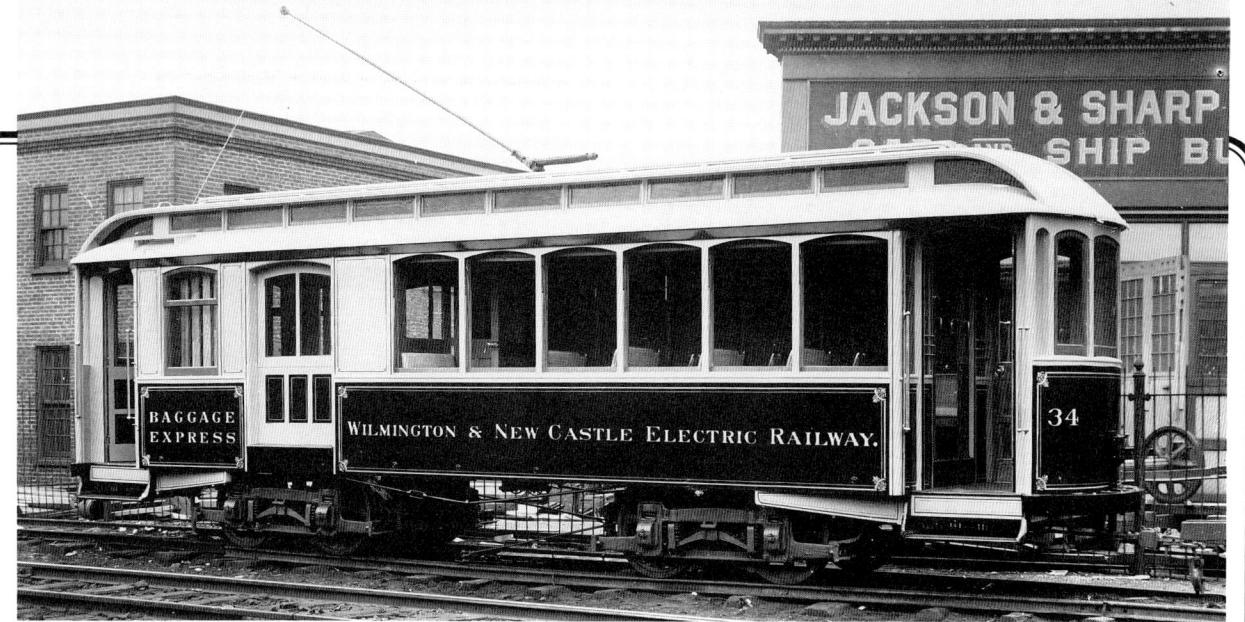

↑In the early years of interurbans, the Jackson & Sharp Company at Wilmington (Del.) was a major car builder. This one was produced in 1901 for the line connecting Wilmington and Delaware City (Del.).

←The interurbans' big growth era (1901–1908) belonged to arch-window wood combos like Puget Sound Electric Railway #516 at Renton Jct. (Wash.). CHARLES A. SMALLWOOD COLLECTION VIA GEORGE KRAMBLES

↓Interurban passenger cars built later had all-steel bodies. Combine #1710 of the Des Moines & Central Iowa Railroad loads express at Perry station on July 5, 1947. CHARLES D. SAVAGE, ROY G. BENEDICT COLLECTION

brought your dog, "chained and properly muzzled." You paid a charge for the dog, often the same amount as an adult fare.

This type of interurban car, a *combination passenger and baggage car,* became so familiar that it was just called a *combine* (pronounced "COM-byn") or *combo.* The last new combines were built in 1948, the front-end cars of new streamliners for the Illinois Terminal Railroad. In 1954 the Potomac Edison Company replaced combine trolleys between Frederick and Thurmont (Md.) with a combine *bus!* Like electric railway vehicles everywhere, they carried "not only passengers."

At the beginning of the streetcar era, most communication was local within one city. Telephones were not widely used. You could send a telegram and the Western Union messenger on his bicycle would deliver it, but most people reserved that method for emergencies. Even a 1¢ postal card mailed in the morning received afternoon delivery within the city. We don't need that kind of mail service today because phone calls give closer communication and are cheaper (relative to inflation).

A few lines including the Miami Beach (Fla.) Railway brought the corner letter box to every corner along the car line by mounting one on the dash of the car. But stopping a passing streetcar to mail a letter never became widespread.

Carriers with their heavy leather letter bags rode ordinary streetcars free to reach their routes from their branch post offices. But in bulk, most local mail was carried in post office wagons. Powered transportation could save time and insure that "neither snow nor rain nor heat nor gloom of night stays these couriers

Chapter **3** T

Mail moved on electric railways in closed pouches and in Railway Post Office cars.

↑**The clerk's apartment in Philadelphia Rapid Transit Company RPO #2084.** PRT, ROBERT L. PRESBREY COLLECTION

from the swift completion of their appointed rounds." Besides, putting the mail aboard a special streetcar would allow some of the sorting to be done while in transit, further speeding service. Of course this was not a new idea, only an application of the *Railway Post Office* (RPO) as used on intercity steam trains for decades.

It was first tried on streetcars in 1891 at St. Louis. This was early enough that a few cable lines had mail trailers. The RPO cars, routed to reach branch post offices, ran as often as hourly. Along the way the clerk emptied letter boxes and accepted mail posted in a slot in the side of the car. Eventually 15 U. S. cities used this method.

Painted white with gleaming gold lettering, the streetcar RPO's stood out from ordinary streetcars which were then dark green in most cities. Some streetcar managements considered them insurance against carmen's strikes and against track obstruction by slow-moving drays. Labor wouldn't interfere with the United States mails! The RPO's were clearly the glamour vehicles of the streetcar companies. However, glamour couldn't get them through the congestion of passenger streetcars in central cities nor eliminate delays to all traffic when

they stood at downtown intersections to transfer mail pouches between routes. Improved motor trucks in the second decade of the new century wiped out the mail cars. Other than for ceremonial occasions, the last of them ran in Baltimore in 1929.

The interurbans had RPO's just as the railroads did. Many routes were scheduled only once a day, except Sundays (but including holidays, unlike the usual transit practice of running the same service on holidays as on Sundays). They could reach towns not tapped by railroads, especially after reductions in local railroad passenger service in the 1920's.

An interurban RPO started in 1895 between Williamsburgh and Northampton (Mass.) on the Northampton Street Railway, but some routes began late in the life of the interurban industry. The last interurban RPO ran between Los Angeles and San Bernardino on the Pacific Electric Railway (1947–1950)— only 27 years before the last railroad RPO. There were only about thirty interurban RPO routes in the entire nation (not all at the same time) and many major interurbans such as the West Penn Railways, the Piedmont & Northern Railway and the North Shore Line never had one. The Saanich line of the British Columbia

↑**Under the trainshed of the Indianapolis Traction Terminal, the Peru & Indianapolis RPO operated by the Indiana Railroad loads up at 5:25 AM on July 4, 1938.** JOHN F. HUMISTON

Newspapers

Before radio broadcasting in the 1920's and especially television, which became widespread about 1950, people were big consumers of newspapers. Since electric railways ran where the metropolitan population was located, newspapers were transported in bulk by electric cars. In big cities that meant several competing daily papers (morning and afternoon), foreign-language papers, law bulletins and racing forms.

Bulky and slow-loading, this freight was not well adapted to passenger streetcars. But in some cities, old cars carried loads from a stop near the newspaper printing plant to outlying distribution points. Tire conservation in World War II even meant a brief resurgence. Newspaper cars had to follow cars making passenger stops at every corner. Trucks owned by the publishers easily replaced this form of movement as they could make better time. The news is perishable!

Carrying newspapers by rail was viable later on suburban runs where point-to-point average speed was better. The Cleveland Interurban Railroad took papers to Shaker Heights (Ohio) in less than half an hour. Suburban trains on steam railroads (including their electrified suburban districts) got a big share of this traffic, especially the afternoon papers on trains at the early part of the commuter rush hour. Interurban lines met the same need and had hourly departures throughout the midday and the ability to deliver to stops too small for railroad service. These advantages were so great that even an interurban whose city terminal was at an outlying point such as the end of a car line could get the business. The publishers would truck the papers to the interurban railhead.

The newspapers rode in the baggage compartment of combines, in the cab or elsewhere, sometimes even on passenger seats! Some railways would obstruct the vestibules while others recognized that as a hazard. A few trains

Electric Railway out of Victoria (B. C.) featured mail cars from about 1913 to 1924.

Interurban RPO's were always mail *apartments* in the cars. No route had enough density for full RPO cars. The post office contracted for apartments of specific size, usually 15 feet long and the width of the car, and the railways furnished the vehicles. Many of the cars carried the regulation catcher arm as on steam railroad RPO's, but it had no use where trains plodded through town streets. Mail was taken by hook at Spokane Bridge (Wash.) station on the Spokane, Coeur d'Alene & Palouse Railway, perhaps the only interurban to do so. The RPO of the San Francisco, Napa & Calistoga Railway was conventional while on the interurban car, but at the Vallejo (Calif.) wharf the clerk, his supplies and the mail transferred to a portable apartment. Then it was wheeled onto a ferry for the trip to San Francisco.

In both the U. S. and Canada, far more common than RPO's was *closed-pouch mail.* Canvas mail bags were carried without a postal clerk in attendance. Indeed they were taken by railway employees to and from post offices up to ¼ mile from rail stations. The pouches went in the baggage compartment along with checked baggage and express or on some roads just lay on the floor by the motorman's feet.

By this means over a hundred city streetcar lines became mail routes, some as early as 1887. So did many interurban railways—perhaps a majority of them—though often not terminal-to-terminal, only to and from intermediate post offices not served by local railroad trains. Since the mail had to reach every place, not just the big cities, a town of only a few hundred people might get a mail pouch for itself or for transfer by highway to off-line communities. The bus successors of some interurban railway routes continued their closed-pouch mail business.

In the modern era, transit service still has advantages for moving mail. In the 1990's Express Mail between Oakland (Calif.) and Fremont, Hayward and San Leandro is routed via trains of the Bay Area Rapid Transit District. About 300 pieces of this high-rated mail are carried daily by messengers (Postal Service employees) riding the trains.

were only for papers, especially morning papers when few passenger runs were scheduled.

Carrier agencies in interurban towns received their bundles of papers from the motorman. For them speed meant bypassing the station baggage room. Off-line agencies sent vans to town or even to convenient crossroad interurban stops. Neighborhood stores that sold papers got smaller bundles. At country stops carrier boys got enough papers for their routes. Each bundle was addressed with a label showing the railroad name, train time, delivery station and consignee. Some interurban roads billed the newspaper publishers at intervals while others required prepayment in the form of tickets stuck to each bundle.

On the high-speed lines, carrying the news came into its own! Bundles of papers were timed off the press to meet a Limited even if the papers were for local points. The motorman showed his skill and timing by holding down the controller and whistling for crossings with one hand while throwing newspaper bundles out the window with the other. His target wasn't just anywhere in the village, either. The traffic manager would hear about it if the papers rolled into a muddy ditch! It was better to aim them right into the open-faced shelter shed. People waiting for locals knew that they had better step out into the rain when they heard a Limited coming! Broken boards in the back of the shed proved that the motormen found their mark.

This kind of operation wouldn't be tolerated today, but electric railways aren't in the newspaper business today. Most of the interurbans lost their market share and ceased operation before the newspapers did. In the days of large train crews commuter railroads had the flagman throw off the papers. Later they increased crew productivity by dropping the flagman and carrying "only passengers." But once, the electric railways had carried the news too.

↑This one dairy received more than 75% of the Philadelphia & West Chester Traction Company's milk. It switched to trucks in late 1924; that resulted in the end of all freight on the railway the following year.
D. SARGENT BELL, RONALD DEGRAW COLLECTION

↓Milk rode on a ticket. Empty cans returned on another coupon or "on their initials." JOSEPH M. CANFIELD

FONDA, JOHNSTOWN & GLOVERSVILLE R. R. CO.

TEN GALLONS CREAM

14785

To

This coupon will be detached from ticket by train Baggageman or Conductor and forwarded to General Auditor.

Most interurban railways reached farm districts and had one end anchored in a sizable city. This meant that they could bring in milk and cream. Even with a wagon transfer to the city dairy, they could get the traffic. During the interurban era, labor for transloading was plentiful and cheap in American cities.

The raw milk moved in uninsulated, unrefrigerated 10-gallon metal cans owned by the farmers. They put it on a wooden platform just a few feet square at car-floor height within reach of both the interurban track and the crossroad. There the cans waited, unattended,

Chapter 4 From Dai

Milk went to the city market on many interurban railways.

for the morning milk run. In some places sheds kept the sun off, but timekeeping was so precise that this was usually unnecessary.

Most lines had too much milk to carry it in the baggage compartment of a combine. This was *mass* transportation because all cows are milked at the same hour! Usually the milk run was a box motor. The milk train of the British Columbia Electric Railway, three cars, handled 475 cans a day. Serving a newly developed farming country, it brought the cans back filled with water for farms that didn't yet have wells.

As a typical move by rail of only 10–50 miles was completed in a couple of hours, no refrigeration was required. A few interurban lines had bulk milk tank cars but most did not enjoy concentrated enough traffic.

Some interurbans saw their milk traffic erode as early suburbanization built up portions of the farm regions they reached. Improvements in motor trucks and hard roads of course took the traffic away from some of the longer-lived lines because trucks gave direct farm-to-dairy service. Yet the Illinois Terminal Railroad still carried some milk in the 1950's. The North Shore Line had milk tickets in stock in the 1960's but they had been unused for some years. Most interurbans retained the business until their general unprofitability caused their abandonment.

Farm to City Dairy

↑From farms around Ephrata, Mount Joy, Lebanon, Lancaster and countless other towns in the Pennsylvania Dutch countryside, five thousand 10-gallon milk cans daily travelled down Chocolate Avenue via Hershey (Pa.) Transit Company's well-kept dark green express motors.

←On September 5, 1934, ice car #222 at Newport News (Va.) is prominent in "healthy" white paint. It operated from here to Buckroe Beach. JAMES P. SHUMAN

→Car #2607 pauses at 15th and Huntingdon streets in front of Baker Field, the Phillies ball park. It's June 20, 1908 and Philadelphia Rapid Transit Company is new to the freight business. PRT, JOHN GIBB SMITH, JR. COLLECTION

→The milk platform at Castle Rock (Pa.) almost overflows with cans, some shaded under wet blankets. Is it efficient for so many people each to bring a relatively small amount of milk to the car stop? RONALD DEGRAW COLLECTION

Ice

At the beginning of the electric railway era, ice was *the* refrigerant for perishables. In the northern half of the United States it was obtained by cutting it from frozen lakes and moving it to an *ice house,* an insulated building, from which it was shipped year around. Fortunate was an interurban railway that had a lake up the line from its major city! In the 1920's an ice house along the Mason City (Ia.) & Clear Lake Railroad sent out as many as fifty refrigerator car loads on summer days. Even as late as 1933, flat cars with sideboards brought ice into town over the Winnipeg, Selkirk & Lake Winnipeg Railway in Manitoba.

The Kentucky Traction & Terminal Company operated an ice *motor* to outlying towns from the ice-making plant of the Lexington Ice Company. This was a "family" operation as both companies were Insull subsidiaries. The Newport News (Va.) Distilled Ice Company peddled its product from cars on the Newport News & Hampton Railway, Gas & Electric Company, which owned most of its stock.

Mechanical refrigeration of cold-storage warehouses and electric refrigerators in homes were making inroads on natural ice by the 1930's. Because of these devices, the shipping of ice became only a memory.

↑The Lehigh Valley Transit Company, running until 1951, was the last line to handle LCL but not carload interchange with railroads. Its #C2 loads at Sellersville (Pa.) station. RAILWAYS TO YESTERDAY, INC.—H. P. SELL COLLECTION

Several forms of freight traffic have already been described and more will follow, but on most interurbans the greatest traffic (other than passengers) was *less-than-carload* freight (LCL). Some roads called it *merchandise dispatch* or other names. The steam railroads also handled "Elsie L" but for them carloads were the greater part of the traffic. Most interurban railways did not have much carload business.

LCL consisted of goods moving as individual pieces or packaged. At one time wooden barrels were common packaging for small items—even bottled beer. Barrels were reasonably strong and could be moved by tilting and rolling them. Some things including sugar went in cloth bags. During the interurban era, corrugated cardboard boxes came into use. Pottery, plate glass and many other things travelled in wooden boxes. The crates sometimes weighed over 800 pounds. Large unbreakable pieces of freight like stoves were sent unpackaged, just with a shipping tag tied on.

Most LCL was outbound from major city terminals. However, a number of lines built up inbound traffic in fresh fruit. A few cars a night might be filled with small lots for sale the next morning in the city or even at farmers' markets at intermediate towns. As with milk, quick transit on the interurbans made refrigeration unnecessary. However, ventilation was important. The Southern Michigan Railway, after wrecking an enclosed car, used a fruit motor with slatted racks instead of a carbody at one end. Ordinary box cars were adequate, though.

The greatest traffic on most interurbans, besides passengers, was less-than-carload freight.

↑**At Hershey (Pa.) Square, candy is transferred from a truck to Hershey Transit Company box motor #25. It is going to Lebanon via another truck connection from Palmyra.** RICHARD H. STEINMETZ, STEPHEN D. MAGUIRE COLLECTION

→**Standard-gauge Lehigh Valley Transit Company express motor #C2 unloads at Chestnut Hill station, circa 1913. The freight will continue via the Philadelphia Rapid Transit Company's broad-gauge freight cars.** RAILWAYS TO YESTERDAY, INC.— H. P. SELL COLLECTION

rels, Bags and Boxes

The Los Angeles–Pacific Railroad brought lemons into Los Angeles from orchards at Hollywood around the turn of the century. Butter and eggs also went to city wholesalers. In some places meat was carried from city packing plants to outlying communities. The pleasant aroma of warm bread fresh from city bakeries is a favorite memory of many people who experienced interurbans.

In the 'teens, the *Electric Railway Journal* advised: "Small urban stores or shops do not want to carry a large stock, and it is for their interest to wait until the last minute before placing an order for a new supply." Then they could get their goods quickly via interurban. And we think "just-in-time" delivery is a modern management concept!

Many things were being sent to factories, wholesalers or retail stores, but there were also consumer goods billed to individuals. As late as the 1940's Sears catalog orders for the Allentown-Bethlehem region went out from Philadelphia via the Lehigh Valley Transit Company.

A report of losses on the Midwestern network shows the kind of goods that came up "short": a chest of drawers, a roll of "cleaning cloth" going to a hardware dealer, a carton of coffee, a typewriter desk, 24 bags of gear couplings for Delco-Remy, a 238-pound box of General Electric motor parts, two oxygen cylinders, galvanized pipe in bundles, a radio and tubes, a gasoline kitchen range, an electric refrigerator and parts, four dozen shovels and a washing machine. More items were "short" than "over." Anecdotal evidence holds that cigarette shipments were targeted for theft while in transit. The security of the cars while on the road was just another of the duties of the train crew. Those men used elementary methods to discourage opportunities for theft.

LCL was loaded onto the cars by railway employees at a city *freight house* located in a manufacturing district close to downtown. Shippers' wagons or trucks or commercial drayage firms brought the goods to a platform alongside the driveway. The best freight houses boasted granite block driveways whose rough surface provided good traction for horseshoes! Loads were taken off the drays onto the freight house floor, where they were weighed.

↓In 1915 Bay State Street Railway carried so many shoes that even its freight cars came in pairs—22 of its 39 express motors had multiple-unit control. Much of the business from plants such as this one at Brockton (Mass.) was transferred at Providence (R. I.) to boats en route New York City. GENERAL ELECTRIC, NORTON D. CLARK COLLECTION

↑The Bay State's Harrison Avenue freight station in Boston, 1913, a long way from today's automated truck terminal! O. R. CUMMINGS COLLECTION

↓The finishing touches were still being applied to the Harrison Avenue freight station in early 1912 when this photograph was made. O. R. CUMMINGS COLLECTION

Then the freight was loaded onto cars arranged along a platform on the opposite side of the house. At large freight houses, cars were spotted on two or more parallel tracks with the further ones being loaded by carrying the freight right through the nearer cars. Steel *gangplanks* for bridging the gaps were a stock item around freight houses. In such a layout the cars and drays stood outdoors. Loading was protected from rain only by the roof overhang. Completely enclosed stations existed in fewer cities.

Moving the freight by muscle power with two-wheelers or on platform carts was heavy work! It produced personal injuries to the warehousemen. A surviving record for one small freight house shows 12 injury cases while handling freight over the course of seven years.

→Lehigh Valley Transit Company #C4 at North Front Street freight house in Allentown (Pa.), circa 1914, with Autocar electric trucks of the Adams Express Company. When the batteries were practically dead, the railway towed the trucks in for recharging. RAILWAYS TO YESTERDAY, INC.—H. P. SELL COLLECTION

↓Box trailer #696 and truck #38 (used for city pick-up and delivery) exchange a bulky but light load of insulation at the Muncie freight house, February 13, 1939. JAMES F. COOK, GEORGE KRAMBLES COLLECTION

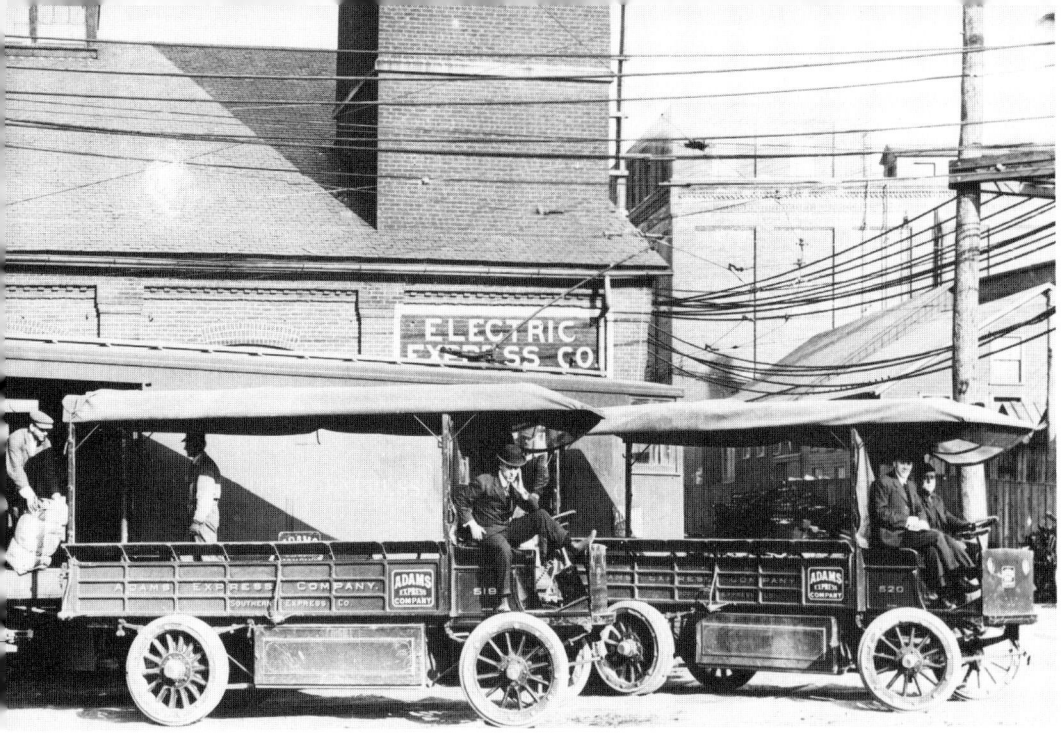

↓Ellery S. Dunbar stands next to a pile of groceries. It was a less comfortable era—"Uncle Ike" wears a tie with his overalls. SHOEMAKER

↑**Pacific Electric Railway uses Los Angeles Union Passenger Terminal, September 24, 1950.** WILLIAM D. MIDDLETON

↓**Peaches go into Union Street Railway #303 at Island Park near Fall River (Mass.).** O. R. CUMMINGS COLLECTION

A very few of the big, longer-surviving inter-urbans introduced fork-lift trucks.

In the office at the front of the shed or up-stairs, clerks prepared waybills for each individual shipment. At many stations the waybills were filled by hand, maybe none too legibly! This lighter work was also very labor-intensive.

Interline moves required *transloading* from one car to another at the freight house in the junction city. In the 1920's some interurban railways added trucks or made traffic agreements with intercity truck lines, either to bridge gaps in the interurban network, to replace abandoned rail routes or to discourage competition with existing lines. This required more handling to transfer the freight at the railhead.

Of course these are the same ideas as with the railways' bus operations. They tried handling "not only passengers" on rubber tires. The trucking was done by the railway company itself, by an obvious subsidiary or by a company that might hide its ownership link while "co-ordinating" the service.

The whole loading process was reversed at the destination freight house. Small cities often had a combination station—a passenger waiting room and ticket office with a freight room alongside a track in back or on a cross street—all arranged to be managed by one agent. The crews of night freights (when the agent was off duty) carried keys to the freight room.

Many interurbans began LCL activity along with the first passenger service. Others, especially those that had grown from purely streetcar systems, saw the need only in response to shippers' requests for service. In Pennsylvania, the electric lines had been chartered as strictly passenger railways though they also carried milk. Here the Homsher Act, a 1907 state law, took precedence and allowed trolley freight to begin with permission of the municipalities.

Originally LCL was handled by the railways only from freight house to freight house. Big shippers and receivers had their own teams. Anyone who didn't hired a commercial carter. Later, pick-up and delivery became common.

In villages the interurbans had no freight facilities and made curbstone delivery. Goods could even be left "at consignee's risk" at country flagstops: "Less Carload [sic] freight delivered on platform only, with shelter house." If you expected a shipment you made an early morning trip to your local stop. Such places terminated LCL but seldom originated any.

Long before overnight air express, the interurbans offered *next morning delivery* along the route of any one train. That is, LCL received in the freight house by a cutoff time, typ-

↓**The more modest city station of the 4½-mile Roby & Northern Railroad at Roby (Tex.). New in 1923 when the line was electrified, it served as the freight outlet for the seat of Fisher County, a cotton, grain and livestock-raising region. Reportedly 115,000 bales of cotton passed over the platform in the rear.** R&N, WILLIAM C. JANSSEN COLLECTION

↑On the Philadelphia & Western Railway in summer 1951, a Lehigh Valley Transit Company freight crosses the Schuylkill at Norristown (Pa.). LESTER K. WISMER

↓Clinton, Davenport & Muscatine Railway #101 in Davenport (Ia.) on August 26, 1938. This car belongs to the 650-volt DC Clinton Division. JAMES P. SHUMAN

↑At West Junction on August 13, 1937, the Milwaukee Electric Railway & Light Company's express motor #M2 with train of three trailers inbound from Watertown (Wis.) meets city car #597 on Route 10, Wells-Downer. Later the Milwaukee system discouraged LCL, diverting it to a truck line in 1941. JAMES P. SHUMAN

ically late afternoon, could be expected at destination the next day. The trains generally moved at night. Operation was six days a week but work was noticeably lighter on Saturdays.

Over longer distances, a hundred miles or so, delivery was second-day or even third-day. The networks of connecting interurban lines were small enough that delivery could be made to any point by the fourth morning.

This was better speed than railroad LCL services provided. Rates were higher in some cases, while other interurban managers saw a competitive advantage in matching or even undercutting railroad rates. It was not as rapid as delivery by express, but by express the heavier loads would have been prohibitively expensive even if they were acceptable. The advertising catch-line EXPRESS SERVICE AT FREIGHT RATES was found throughout the interurban industry, but it may have been a slight exaggeration.

The service was vulnerable to competition. The Eastern Massachusetts (successor to Bay State) Street Railway gave up all freight in 1920. Road development here made intercity trucking feasible that early. But in contrast, the Lehigh Valley Transit Company did a brisk business, unashamedly called trolley freight, until 1951.

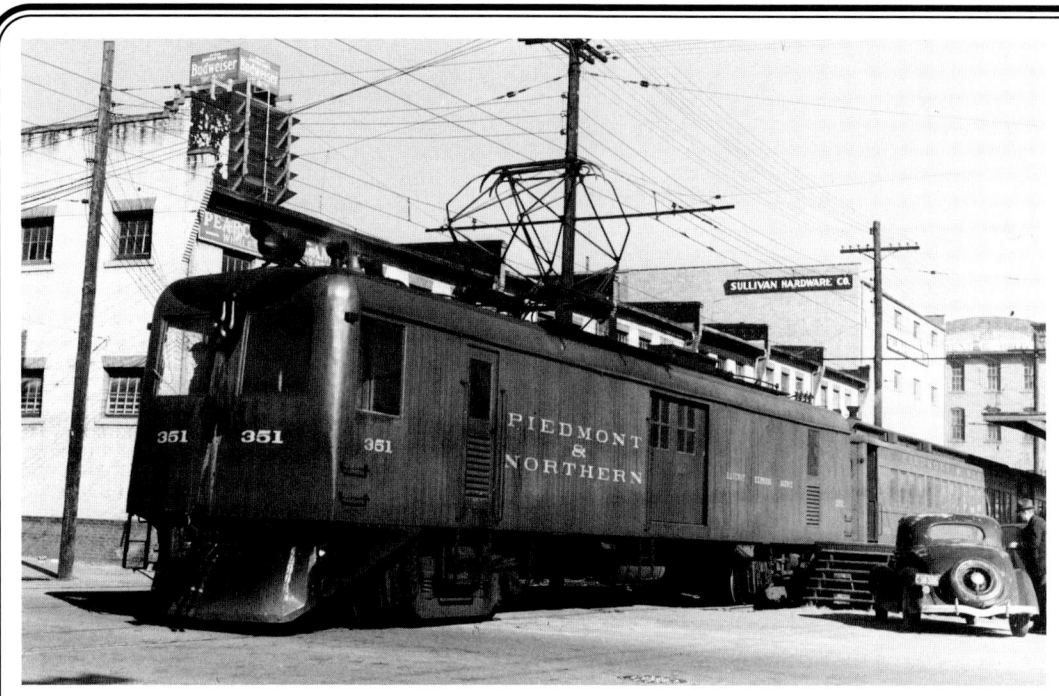

↑Piedmont & Northern Railway #351 leads a passenger train at Greenville (S. C.) on February 8, 1942. WILLIAM C. JANSSEN

Mixed Trains

Some interurban railways, especially the roads in the West that scheduled only a few trains a day "just like the steam railroads," ran their box motors at the head of passenger trains. Typically this operation was permitted by the use of multiple unit control. Other lines tacked a box car on the rear of some passenger trains to handle either local express or car-load freight. Interurban cars were typically so overpowered that a trailer didn't hurt the schedule. However, common box cars were rough-riding at passenger-train speeds; damage could result to shipments packed as if they were traveling by express. Sometimes interurban-type box trailer bodies were mounted on passenger car trucks (without motors) to avoid this problem.

↓The Montreal & Southern Counties Railway needs five cars in this train of June 18, 1947. The express business is being done in motor #502 and trailer #515. At Greenfield Park near Mackayville (Qué). WILLIAM C. JANSSEN

↑On June 29, 1948, a Texas Electric Railway train to Waco leaves Dallas with a trailer. JOHN F. HUMISTON

↓This Salt Lake & Utah Railroad train is mostly for fast freight. CLIFF BRAY, WILLIAM C. JANSSEN COLLECTION

As the cost of labor increased, loading and unloading individual pieces of LCL became grossly uneconomic. Besides, often the railway's cars could not reach a likely destination. Then one or more transfers meant still more expense. At each of these points the goods were exposed to theft. Thus for efficiency alone, the railways had an incentive to handle freight in fewer units and without transfers—if they could find a way.

The way was to load the freight in some kind of a standardized container which could travel by either rail or highway. The *container* could be just a big box—or the entire truck.

The oft-reported first (1894–1895) among electric lines was the Oakland, San Leandro & Haywards (Calif.) Electric Railway, which carried wagons to the East Bay shore from where they continued to San Francisco by boat. In 1910 the Hudson & Manhattan Railroad planned to apply the same idea on a smaller scale to haul baggage. Eight ordinary station baggage carts would be rolled across aprons from the station platform onto a Hudson Tubes car. With unskilled labor still abundant, these developments were before their time.

→As the box motor pulls away from a loading ramp, Railwagons settle down onto Lake Shore Electric Railway flat car #500 to which they are loosely attached. NORMAN CARLSON COLLECTION

Chapter 6 In tl

Several interurban railways in the 1920's and 1930's tried containers or piggyback.

The Motor Terminals Company at Cincinnati was using containers to bring LCL by road from shippers' plants to the steam railroad freight houses. In 1921 it expanded to intermodal carriage of containers via rail cars of the Cincinnati, Lawrenceburg & Aurora Electric Street Railroad. Gantry cranes transferred these 5-ton containers "in five minutes." Motor Terminals containers also moved to Dayton and Toledo (Ohio) via the Cincinnati & Lake Erie Railroad for a few years after 1931.

In 1923 the Detroit United Railway devised a way to get along without overhead cranes. Containers with 9-inch wheels were loaded from motor trucks to rail flat cars using power from the truck engine. Two sizes of containers, for 2½-ton and 5-ton loads, were offered in closed and stake-side form. Later, the Boston & Worcester and Springfield (Mass.) street railways handled containers for the Freight Container Company using similar technology.

Back in Toledo in 1931, the Lake Shore Electric Railway at the other side of town advocated a different approach, highway trailers which could roll on their own two wheels behind tractors over the streets at the terminal cities rather than requiring a separate flatbed truck chassis. The particular novelty of the Railwagon was its lack of cross axles so that it could be carried with its wheels astride a narrow flat car. The idea had been conceived thirty-some years earlier by Col. Joseph C. Bonner. In the 1931 application, a ramp arrangement permitted the Railwagon to be parked over a track at the railhead and later mounted on the car with no truck driver in attendance.

Two of the Chicago area interurbans were already carrying trailers but driving them off and on the cars via a ramp up to car-floor height at the end of a spur track. At first, in 1926, the trailers were captive fleets specially designed for attachment to rail cars. These trailers would carry 8 tons each. Later the tie-down method was changed so that any truck trailer could be accommodated and as such, the

North Shore Line operated until 1947. Advertising its "new ferry truck service" in a 1931 timetable, the South Shore Line said: "Tractor-drawn trailers are spotted at the consignor's plant, picked up in the afternoon by the railroad, and delivered the following morning at consignee's plant."

The amount of solicitation needed to get and keep this competitive traffic was beyond the means of any ordinary interurban line. Of course it was doomed by abandonment of railways of which it was only a small part.

But the same concept gained a foothold on a few railroads in 1936. Finally in the 1950's it saw widespread acceptance as *piggyback*. Perhaps the biggest surprise in the way the railroads have developed it is today's total reliance on loading by crane. With no *circus style loading*, bridge plates are no longer required to span the gap between cars.

At the same time, intermodal (truck, rail or ship) containers have become the center of a highly visible revolution in freight transportation. Nowadays "small" containers accommodate 25 tons. Are they really a modern idea? Some shippers around Cincinnati thought so—seventy years ago!

↓In 1931 The Milwaukee Electric Railway & Light Company found a hard way to carry containers—*inside* a box car. They were transferred via "slip rails" on the car floor and truck bed, using power from a winch. "TM" had considerable interurban bus-rail transfer, so this extended intermodal service to "not only passengers." TM, ROBERT W. WIETZKE COLLECTION

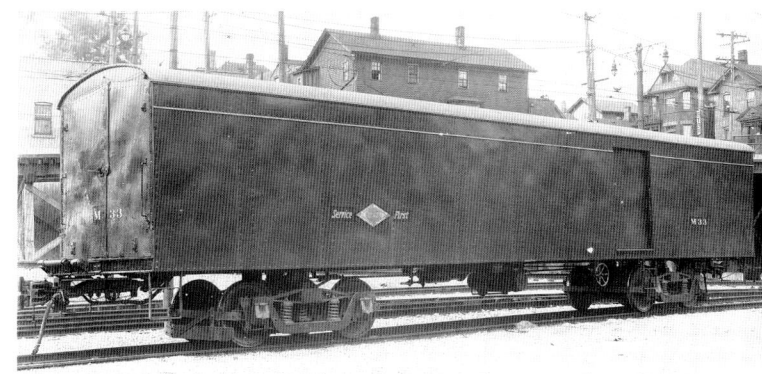

Name of Efficiency

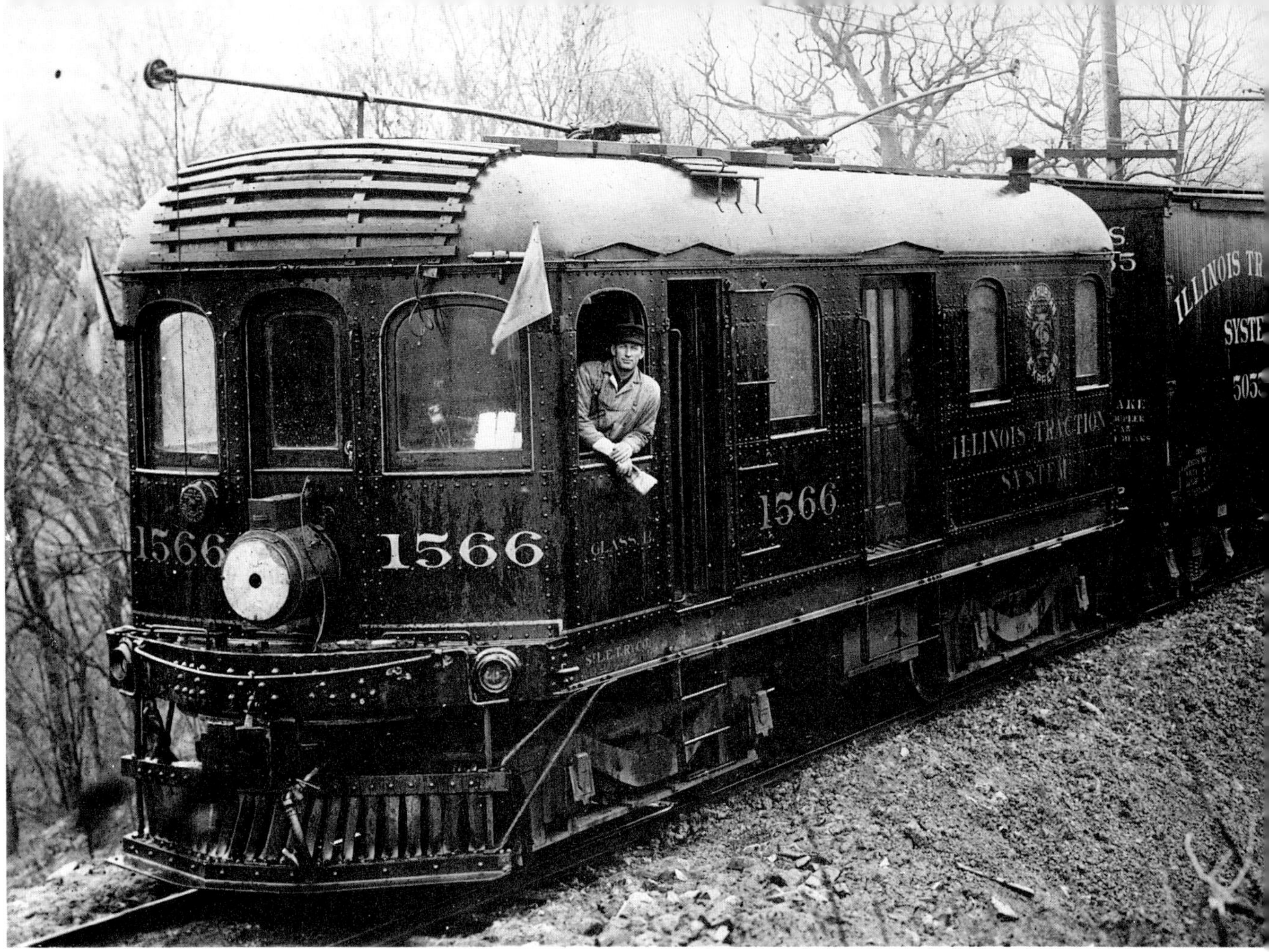

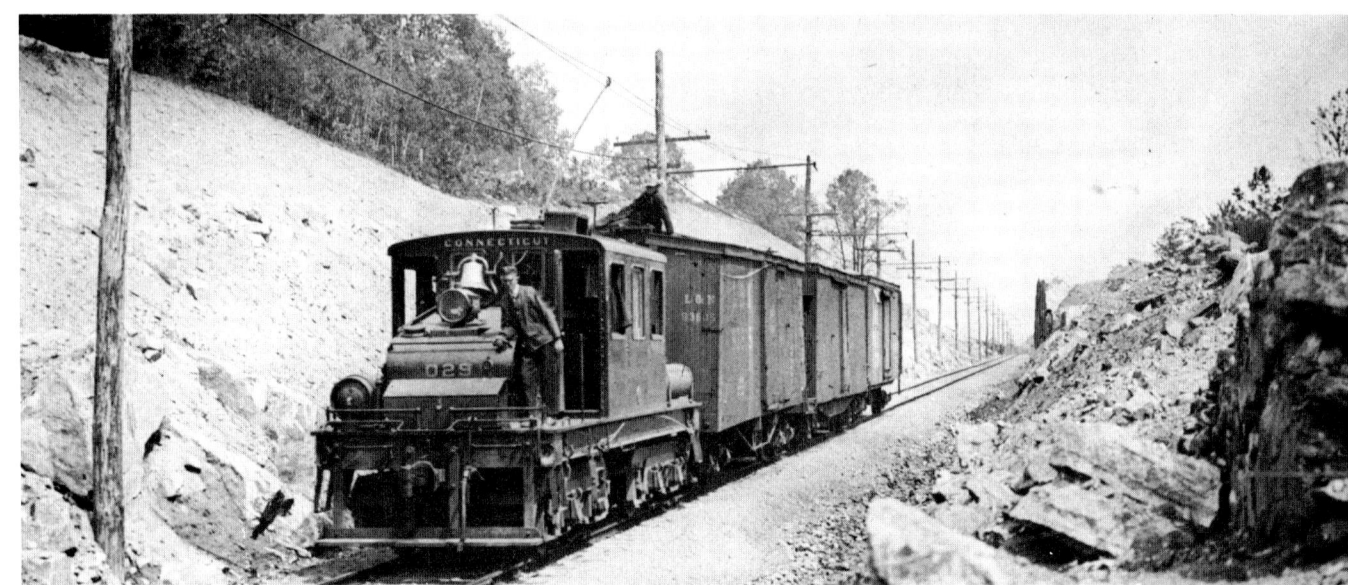

↑**Illinois Traction System boasted of this 25-car grain train.** ITS, WILLIAM C. JANSSEN COLLECTION

↓**On June 12, 1913, the Connecticut Company hauls up Chase grade near Waterbury.** NORTON D. CLARK COLLECTION

Chapter 7 Pul

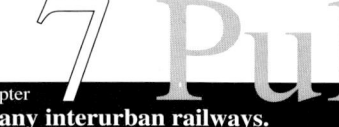

Freight in carloads—mainly in the red box cars of steam lines—was significant on many interurban railways.

The traffic already discussed is less-than-carload lots. That was the greater part of the electric railways' freight. However, on some interurban roads there was also a great amount of *carload* traffic. Later LCL went predominantly by truck. By the early 1950's all electric railway freight was carloads.

Carload traffic could be handled in traction-style cars such as box trailers restricted to the electrics. Where line limitations such as track curvature, clearances and strength of bridges were not too great, the interurbans could use railroad-style cars, even railroad-owned cars. Some roads hauled both types of cars in the same train. The Wilkes-Barre & Hazleton (Pa.) Railway would even handle priority loads in passenger trains. Of course those electric roads that were built to non-standard track gauges (anything other than 4′8½″ between the railheads) could do no railroad *interchange*. Besides gauge, common features of railroad cars include general dimensions, couplers, air brakes and *safety appliances* such as ladders.

↓**Car #20 of the Galt, Preston & Hespeler Street Railway in the Grand River valley of Ontario heads a short train of interchange cars from the States.** R. F. CORLEY COLLECTION

ng the Red Box Cars

←On July 17, 1933, box-cab locomotive #2 of Potomac Edison Company works on Patrick Street, Frederick (Md.). The motorman is running "blind." JOHN J. BOWMAN, JR., JAMES P. SHUMAN COLLECTION

←On August 7, 1934, the New Haven interchange in Linwood (Mass.) is being switched by Taunton-built locomotive #3 of the Whitin Machine Works. This line was electric until 1943. NORTON D. CLARK

←Kansas City Public Service Company is using its Differential dump car #0023 as a locomotive along the Dodson car line in the southern part of Kansas City (Mo.). TERENCE W. CASSIDY COLLECTION

↑**Near the University of Alabama spur in Tuscaloosa, Alabama Power Company box-cab locomotive #101 handles a few railroad cars. Around the time of this December 1, 1941 photo, the railroads used almost 50,000** *ventilated box cars* **like that Louisville & Nashville unit, primarily to carry fruits and vegetables.** C. L. SIEBERT JR.

The typical interurban railway had *local* freight both originating and terminating on its own line. If it developed interchange, it could handle *terminating* freight to consignees on the electric. Fewer interurbans had much *originating* business which they sent off-line via steam-road connections. Still fewer electric lines with multiple interchange points went after the *bridge* or *overhead* business of handling cars between one steam-road connection and another. Bridge traffic could be important for suburban roads around major railroad centers. If they hustled, they could take a car from one railroad to another faster than those roads could inter-

→**Another box-cab in the South, the Piedmont & Northern Railway's #5105 is switching cars in Greenville (S. C.) on this September 28, 1940.** WILLIAM C. JANSSEN

change it directly in their congested city yards. The Chicago, Aurora & Elgin Railroad in 1937 had 12% local, 35% terminating, 8% originating and 45% bridge carloads. The Rochester (N. Y.) subway had half bridge traffic.

Most electric railways with interchange business were interurbans. However, the Key System in the San Francisco East Bay region, not an interurban in the classic sense, had a great deal of interchange with steam roads and with the Sacramento Northern interurban. Some purely city lines, as at Oshawa and Cornwall (Ont.), built up substantial traffic in short switching moves to factories. Industrial regions had compact freight-only switching lines such as the Hoboken (N. J.) Shore Road. A private warehouse choosing an electric switcher rather than a steamer might save on insurance.

On railroads generally and on the interurbans that interchanged freight with them, box cars were the most common car type. Moving with the doors closed and sealed, box cars gave no hint of the nature of their load,

though the traffic patterns of an individual railroad or a region could be a clue. *Most* box cars gave no hint, that is! If a tanning plant was the destination, you knew it by the stench even before you noticed the old low-grade box car assigned to carry hides.

When a box car was standing on an industry's *private siding,* the big painted sign on the factory wall gave a clue to the contents. Canning plants shipped product and also received cartons from the box makers. Lumber went in box cars—a few electric railways were in logging regions, some served lumber mills, and others terminated traffic at retail lumber yards throughout cities and towns. The Lewiston, Augusta & Waterville (Me.) Street Railway noticed that lumber from wood lots moved in winter when it could be brought to the line by sled. Similarly, carloads of brick or tile were handled from kilns or terminating.

Anything produced or consumed in a region went by box car. As early as 1915, country elevators on the Illinois Traction System

↓Two merchandise despatch motors of the Chicago North Shore & Milwaukee Railway, working in multiple unit, haul an impressive northbound freight train through the north side of Waukegan (Ill.) on a bleak afternoon in January 1948. Many of these cars will be interchanged with the Milwaukee Road at Racine (Wis.). WILLIAM C. JANSSEN

↑Washington & Old Dominion Railway locomotive #50 works just outside the Rosslyn (Va.) yard on February 10, 1940. JAMES P. SHUMAN

↓Pacific Electric Railway steeple-cabs #1628 and #1620 cross the Santa Ana River trestle on the San Bernardino line, October 2, 1949. JOHN E. KOSCHWANEZ

↑**Would you say that this freight train is overpowered? Steeple-cab locomotives #3004 and #3003 of the third-rail Chicago, Aurora & Elgin Railway bring a Union Pacific box car west across Liberty Drive into the Wheaton (Ill.) yards on April 6, 1950.** WILLIAM D. MIDDLETON

shipped 4,000 cars of grain per year, one-sixth of the line's carloads. Wheat or other grains came into mills and left as bagged flour. Sugar refineries also gave a two-way haul—sugar beets in, bags out. Textile or knitting mills were regional specialties. The Galveston-Houston (Tex.) Electric Railway served a cotton compress. The San Francisco, Napa & Calistoga Railway originated grapes and wines; the British Columbia Electric Railway, shingles; the Grafton & Upton (Mass.) Railroad, hats; a line at Minneapolis, ammunition; the Fort Dodge (Ia.) Line after World War II, gypsum.

The alternative to having a private siding was to receive or ship carloads through a *team track*. This was a public interface between rail and highway trucks (originally, horse-drawn wagons, hence the name). Any shipper could truck freight to or from a nearby team track located near an LCL freight house or elsewhere along the rail right-of-way. Shipper forces, unlike railroad personnel as with LCL, transloaded the cargo at team tracks.

↑Motor #8 of the "Traction Company" (Central California Traction Company) hauls a train at X Street in Sacramento on July 12, 1942. W. C. WHITTAKER

↓Locomotive #801 of the South Shore Line is at Olive interchange with the New York Central west of South Bend (Ind.) on June 13, 1966. WILLIAM D. MIDDLETON

←Freight trailer #4 is an ordinary-looking railroad-style box car, right down to the knuckle couplers. Surprisingly, such a car belonged to a New England line: the Bangor (Me.) Railway & Electric Company. It was built in 1915 by American Car & Foundry Company. O. R. CUMMINGS

↑Van Dorn couplers limit #209 to haulage behind electric cars equipped the same way. But this railway's "Pennsylvania gauge" (5'2½") was the *real* limitation! Express car of the Harmony Route (Pittsburgh, Harmony, Butler & New Castle Railway) is at Butler (Pa.) in 1918. FRED W. SCHNEIDER COLLECTION

←Another nonstandard coupler (this time a Tomlinson) and also jumper receptacles for trainlines allow this car to be used between motor cars in a multiple-unit train (as you can see on page 28). On April 14, 1946, Montreal & Southern Counties Railway #515 is at St. Lambert (Qué.). H. L. GOLDSMITH

Railroad-style Cars of Interurbans

Some fifty interurbans owned about 8,000 railroad-style cars. Such cars ran only on the straighter interurban track—they couldn't be wrapped around the courthouse square. Some were restricted to home-road use; others were widely interchanged like any railroad car. A few fleets were far bigger than the road's passenger rosters. The Fort Dodge, Des Moines & Southern Railroad's 2,500 "gray backs" stood out among the usual dull red of railroad box cars. In 1925 the Pacific Electric Railway owned over 3,000 railroad freight cars. The Illinois Terminal Railroad purchased 1,200 box cars and about 300 other freight units in the late 1940's. Other lines had anywhere from none to a thousand. The Iowa Traction Railroad is the last electric whose *reporting marks,* IATR, appear in interchange—on 128 cars in 1991. Owned by GE Railcar Services, these cars are available free to IATR and produce revenue for GE when used elsewhere.

→Car #1118 displays an advance in car construction: steel ends. Note the Fox pressed steel trucks, found on some American railroad freight cars including quite a number owned by Quebec Railway, Light & Power Company. At Québec City, May 25, 1951. H. L. GOLDSMITH

↓Car 1024 of the Cedar Valley Road (Waterloo, Cedar Falls & Northern Railroad) is called an automobile car because of its double doors giving a wider opening. JOSEPH M. CANFIELD

↓Illinois Terminal Railroad #8316 sports steel ends and double-width steel doors. The handbrake on the car end rather than above the roof often accompanied an improved brake valve required on new cars after 1933 and refitted to old ones. Modern trucks also appear; after 1940 arch bar trucks could not be interchanged. JOSEPH M. CANFIELD

Not all carloads were in box cars. In the 1920's and 1930's the states built hard roads through the transportation corridors that the interurbans had developed thirty years earlier. These projects brought the interurbans traffic in sand, gravel and cement. Perhaps the last big road project in which interurbans participated was the Illinois Tollway in 1958. By then the Chicago, Aurora & Elgin Railway was freight-only yet had to lengthen a country siding to accommodate increased carloadings.

To build a concrete bridge or new two-lane highway from thousands of 94-pound bags of cement, first put up a platform at car-floor height along a rural sidetrack. Use tarpaulins for protection from rain squalls. Open the cement bags into wheelbarrow-type hopper carts. Dump them into trucks from a wing of the platform overhanging a driveway in low terrain. Deliver the last few miles to the work face on rubber tires. The methods, while labor-intensive, used gravity where they could. The whole installation was crude, needed for only a season

or two until the paving site moved beyond easy trucking distance. Of course, several interurbans directly served cement plants so that they could originate traffic for many years.

Material for paving city streets (usually the responsibility of the streetcar company under the franchises by which it used the streets) moved in dump cars or on flat cars, perhaps with low board sides to help contain a load.

Nor was such business only for constructing paved roads. In 1918–1921 the Hydro-Electric Power Commission of Ontario built an 8½-mile canal to divert part of the flow of Niagara Falls to a new power house. On a temporary electric railway using standard interurban technology, it used 24 electric locomotives to haul earth away to disposal sites. Excavated rock was broken up to use in concrete. The cement for the concrete gave the nearby Niagara, St. Catharines & Toronto Railway about 10,000 carloads.

Stone, sand, clay and gravel moved in gondola or dump cars. They could be loaded into the cars from *truck dumps*. Trucks backed up on top of a wooden trestle alongside the siding.

↓**Cement has been brought to Lawrence (Ind.) over the Cincinnati & Lake Erie and Indiana railroads (an all-interurban haul) for a road-paving job in 1932. The box cars are C&LE's.** EDWIN P. BELKNAP COLLECTION

↓**The major industry on the Kansas City Kaw Valley Railroad was a cement plant four miles east of Bonner Springs (Kans.). The local lumber dealer is getting a carload.** DONALD E. SMITH, TERENCE W. CASSIDY COLLECTION

Chapter 8 Dig

Electric railways often moved bulk materials for highway construction or other purposes.

42 • *Not Only Passengers*

→Near Muncie, gravel for concrete has been unloaded from side-dump cars right on the Indiana Railroad main. Only box cars for the cement are in the distant spur track. EDWIN P. BELKNAP COLLECTION

→On September 28, 1947, stone blocks ride the Canadian National flat car coupled to British Columbia Electric Railway locomotive #992. ERNIE PLANT, W. C. WHITTAKER COLLECTION

→This apparition is car #109, the side-dump gravel motor of the Wisconsin Power & Light Company. It's hauling more gravel in some side-dump gondola trailers. JOHN DRIVER

ng Their Own Grave

↑**Indiana Railroad coal car #1091 dumps stone from a temporary trestle at 38th Street, Indianapolis, for a highway and bridge construction project.** EDWIN P. BELKNAP COLLECTION VIA JOSEPH M. CANFIELD

When sand was mined by hydraulic dredges, it was loaded wet. Some loads of rock were received at crusher plants.

A few electric railways directly serving quarries carried big stone blocks on flat cars. The Emigration Cañon Railroad was built for this traffic into Salt Lake City (Utah).

These products moved short distances because they were produced throughout the country. It was economic to carry them as much as possible by rail rather than in the small motor trucks on the narrow highways of the day. Many a haul was local on a single interurban

↓**Hard to imagine that a local haul of sand within a city—less than five miles—was made by rail. But it was economic to do it because otherwise, horses and wagons or the primitive motor trucks of 1912 would have been needed.** HAROLD E. COX—PRT COLLECTION

railway. On some lines such moves used interurban-style cars not suitable for handling by the steam roads. Other railways owned gondolas just like those on the steam railroads but kept them for on-line traffic. And interchange traffic, where the electric line acted as the terminating or the originating carrier, was also common, usually using cars of the steam roads.

The more substantial electric railways also handled these commodities for their own use. If an interurban was prosperous enough to relocate lines or improve grades, it would surely haul the necessary material by rail. Many an interurban line exploited an on-line gravel pit for track ballast even if not commercially. When labor was cheap, flat cars with sideboards were often used. Shovel the load on, then shovel it off into the track! This method was used on the rapid transit system of the Chicago Transit Authority as late as 1966.

Several lines bought dump cars primarily for distributing cinders or crushed rock for ballasting track, but they were glad to use the cars for revenue loads. In the 1920's the Differential Steel Car Company's line of side-dump cars (motors and trailers) was extensively marketed to electric railways. The American Car & Foundry Company engineered a version of the *Hart Convertible Gondola* for interurban use. These center-dump cars were well adapted for

Ore

Many large open-pit iron mines (as in Minnesota) or copper mines (as in Arizona) had standard-gauge electric railways to carry *tailings*—mine waste or overburden—to a dump site on the company's property and to bring ore to processing plants. These railways used technology like that of the heavier freight-hauling interurbans. However, *side-arm trolleys* engaged an overhead wire to one side of the track so that cars could be loaded from overhead by "steam" shovels. Tracks were shifted frequently to keep up with mining operations. Not common carriers, these single-purpose railways remote from population centers have excited the imagination of few observers of railroads.

spreading ballast and could be made down into flat-bottom gondolas for commercial traffic. Not only that, but the Indiana Railroad collected them from three previous owners and used them in on-line coal trade.

Two cases are known where track was ballasted by "piggyback": one was The Trolley Museum at Kennebunkport (Me.) in 1957, which unloaded a dump truck off the end of a moving flat car. The more exotic example was on the 4′8½″-gauge electric intramural railroad of the Louisiana Purchase International Exposition in 1904. It equipped a flat car with rails to 4′10″ gauge, loaded a side-dump car of the St. Louis Transit Company and hauled this combination behind a steam construction locomotive to place ballast along its tracks!

Sand for traction went out from a central drying plant to carhouses, sometimes in steel tank cars with pneumatic unloading ability, and also to sand boxes on remote street corners where the car crews could refill the sand boxes on their cars.

Urban railways, for example at Montréal, developed traffic in construction materials for buildings. Until the 1920's it was acceptable just to dump the material alongside the car tracks in the middle of the street! It was perhaps less of an obstruction to traffic than the many slow-moving wagons that would have

↑The Portland-Lewiston (Me.) Interurban Railroad hauls ballast on flat cars past the Gray substation with its Baldwin-Westinghouse locomotive #90. O. R. CUMMINGS COLLECTION

been needed to do the job if the tramway had not been used. Even bricks went this way, neatly stacked on flat cars.

Subway extension at Edmonton (Alta.) in the early 1980's used a work train to haul spoil to an outlying landfill along the light rail line. Dump car bodies were fitted locally to the underframes of tank and stock cars bought from the Northern Alberta Railways. To see cargo moved first behind Edmonton Transit System's steeple-cab locomotive and then in a front-end loader is to experience the timelessness of the electric railway scene.

In some more populated places could be found street and interurban railways which carried various products of the mining industry. Ore trains (motor and trail dump cars) operated directly from the mines to a reduction plant via streetcar tracks in Butte (Mont.). Up to 25 cars a day of lead or zinc ore and another 25 of tailings were transported over the Southwest Missouri Railroad. The Birmingham (Ala.) Railway, Light & Power Company hauled little dump trailers of steel-furnace slag to places where it could be used for fill or in concrete.

→On the Appanoose branch of the Southern Iowa Railway, haydite shipping began about 1960. The gray clay or shale product, used to make lightweight building blocks, goes into a Rock Island hopper. ED WOJTAS

↑The Illinois Traction System was a major interurban practically spanning central Illinois. Coal traffic from mines along much of its territory helped the Traction to evolve into a standard railroad. At an early stage, circa 1910, locomotive #1550 pauses with five coal gondolas at Mackinaw Junction. ITS, WILLIAM C. JANSSEN COLLECTION

In the heyday of electric railways, coal was *the* urban fuel. It was used for generating electricity, as it is today, and also for heating. Steam railroads dominated coal transportation—whole systems were built because of this commodity. But electric lines had surprisingly much of the haul.

Hundreds of underground mines had narrow-gauge electric railways. Their coal saw trolley wire and K controllers before it saw daylight. Electrified divisions of steam railroads—the Virginian, the Norfolk & Western and the Pennsylvania—hauled coal from Appalachian mine regions to tidewater or to western connections. These routes, powered by 11,000-volt AC, were full-scale railroads, the opposite end of the spectrum from mine railways. Their counterpart today (1992), at 50,000 volts, is the 81-mile electrification on the Tumbler Ridge (B. C.) branch of BC Rail Ltd., opened in 1984 for coal hauling.

A few self-contained line-haul railroads exist only to move coal from mineheads to processing or shipping points or nearby power plants. The Muskingum Electric Railroad in Morgan County (Ohio), opened in 1968, was the first. Another such line is the Deseret Western Railway near Rangely (Colo.). Some were conceived as test beds for future railroad electrification technology and use automated operation. While successful for their local purpose, they have not generated large-scale electrification of common carrier railroads.

But neither those big heavy-duty railroad electrifications nor the miniature coal-mining railways is the main subject of this book.

Some electric railways of the middle range, the 600-volt DC street and interurban lines, were in coal-producing regions. The Illinois Traction System boasted 300 cars a day from one on-line mine. The Denver & Northwestern Railway, an interurban built to 3′6″ track gauge, brought coal from mines at Leyden (Colo.) directly to the Denver Tramway powerhouse. A third running rail over part of the line also allowed it to handle 4′8½″-gauge cars—sometimes in the same train—for interchange to the Colorado & Southern Railway. The Seattle & Rainier Valley Railroad at Renton (Wash.) and several of the Iowa lines also originated coal. Many in Pennsylvania, handicapped by their 5′2½″ track gauge, did not.

The urban fuel moved by electric railway at various stages of its journey from coal mine to consumer.

Chapter 9

46 • *Not Only Passengers*

↑On August 7, 1934, Connecticut Company #1071 returns to the New Haven docks from the Derby power plant. CHARLES A. DUNCAN, RICHARD L. WONSON COLLECTION

↓Androscoggin & Kennebec Railway loads coal from tidewater at Bath (Me.). In 1915 the line started bringing a textile mill 2,500 tons a year. RICHARD L. WONSON

↓Connecticut Company #2023 moves a 70-ton hopper at East Hartford, August 17, 1937. RICHARD L. WONSON

Most other electric railways hauled coal only near the delivery end of its journey. In the cities, power plants of the 1890's surprisingly weren't always located along railroads. Their fuel demands were small enough to be brought by horse-drawn wagons from the nearest railroad siding. Powered transport using streetcar tracks would be more efficient. The car tracks couldn't accommodate steam railroad cars, so the coal was transferred into street railway units. Sometimes the coal went on little flat cars with sideboards; often, in dump cars, even motorized ones.

Later, new power plants were built with rail access. When interurbans were developed, around 1900–1910, they found no source of enough power outside major cities. Many a line therefore built a power house near its main shop outside a mid-line town. A good site wasn't always next to a steam railroad, so any old work motor hauled coal cars from an interchange a dozen miles away. It was practicable to design this much interurban line to handle steam railroad cars. On some interurbans this was the only steam railroad interchange. In a smaller number of cases, coal was "interchanged" with water carriers rather than rails.

ice in Its Solid Form

↑The wooden roller coaster at Rocky Glen Park near Scranton (Pa.) forms a backdrop for locomotive #401 of the third-rail Lackawanna & Wyoming Valley Railroad. The seven 50-ton-capacity Delaware, Lackawanna & Western Railroad cars must be new—why would coal hoppers otherwise be so clean?

←Bringing coal to the Northern Indiana Public Service Company involved operation over the South Shore Line of 100-car unit trains of "bathtub hoppers." Electric locomotive #802 handles the westbound empties at Wilson siding in Portage (Ind.). FRED LONNES

After passenger service ended, coal-hauling portions might be retained, even keeping trolley power for years. By this time most power plants were under separate ownership from the rail lines. The Piedmont & Northern Railway served major generating stations of the affiliated Duke Power Company, even into the diesel era.

Dozens of interurbans delivered coal in railroad cars to steam heating plants of institutions—colleges, asylums, prisons, waterworks. The first state-owned trolley at Bismarck was equipped to bring coal up the hill from the Northern Pacific Railway to the North Dakota capitol, but no interchange was ever built. In many places on-line mills and factories had steam plants for heating or industrial processes such as canning. Coal moving over streetcar tracks might be a company load going to a carbarn for heating the shop or for car stoves.

The electric railways also handled a great deal of coal for retail sale. Every urban house had a coal furnace and every neighborhood had coal dealers—perhaps one per square mile.

↑Philadelphia Rapid Transit Company had 16 "ash cars." Its #5615 is about to dump a load, probably in South Philadelphia. HAROLD E. COX COLLECTION

Ashes

Burning coal produced ashes—over a carload a day at the Fraser (Ia.) generating station of the Fort Dodge, Des Moines & Southern Railroad. A rural power plant usually had an on-site dump, but hauling ashes away to a dump produced revenue for a few electric railways.

Where outlying areas were in early stages of development, urban lines were big ash handlers, even in less-than-carload lots. It was common to use dump cars built for the purpose, often motor cars because of the difficulty of operating trains in street traffic.

Cinders from heating plants of buildings were the last traffic of the Chicago Tunnel Company's freight subway in 1959.

For that matter, some cities shipped street sweepings and general garbage over street railways. With plenty of draft horses on the streets, even the sweepings had organic content. Car lines in Brooklyn and Chicago had this plentiful, though odorous, business. Starting later than most, in the 1930's the Department of Street Railways at Detroit used three-car trains of Differential dump cars with extended sides to haul 400 cubic yards of garbage a day on a 6½-mile run. The Regina (Sask.) Municipal Railway featured an enclosed structure where trains of four-wheel steel dump trailers took on garbage from wagons. The loads were taken, under tarpaulins, to an incinerator near the city's sewage plant, a 3-mile haul.

Elaborate *coal yards* had trestle tracks for dumping hopper cars and mechanized silos for storing the coal. At other yards, coal was dumped into pits under a side track, just big enough for the receiving end of a portable conveyor, and the storage was in piles in wooden bins behind a brightly painted board fence. The real shoestring operators didn't have even that much equipment, but just specified gondola cars and hired laborers to shovel them out. A parcel of even 6,000 square feet was enough to get into business in a small way. Outside major cities, the coal business was often combined with other enterprises such as selling feed or sand, stone and other building materials.

The coal yards were located along railroads or the town entrances of interurban lines. On many an interurban the coal haul was from a railroad interchange near one town to a yard in another town that had no railroad access. But many electric lines served coal yards even in towns with competing yards on nearby railroads. Coal for heating obviously produced seasonal peaks in traffic.

↑The hay rides car #05 of the Philadelphia & West Chester Traction Company. In 1992 the trolley line operates as the Southeastern Pennsylvania Transportation Authority—but no freight! NORTH JERSEY CHAPTER COLLECTION—NATIONAL RAILWAY HISTORICAL SOCIETY

↓Chester & Derry (N. H.) Railroad's unnumbered home-built freight car pauses at Derry Village with a steam boiler and some general freight. O. R. CUMMINGS

Freight on *flat cars* moved in the open for all to see, or at most under a tarpaulin which showed the outline of the load and made it possible to guess the contents. Items were *tied down* with cables or chains hooked to the stake pockets along the car sides or constrained between blocks nailed to the wooden decks of the cars.

Even if it ordinarily handled no freight, just about any early street railway could come up with a work car to carry a heating boiler to a new school building or other institution. Once a boiler for the Borden condensed milk plant at Albany (N. Y.) was dragged on a skid, using a streetcar for motive power but not actually to carry the load. Frame houses were often moved through urban streets on rollers. On one occasion a streetcar company got into the act and pulled a house for the moving contractor.

The Elmira, Corning & Waverly (N. Y.) Railway operated a Sunday train for a "boat and canoe livery." Canoes were stacked three deep on a flat car. The Purdue University drum should have travelled as baggage over the Terre Haute, Indianapolis & Eastern Traction Company, but being too high for the ceiling of the combines it went on a flat car.

Hauling long (62′) rails for city trackwork was a special problem. The Philadelphia Rapid Transit Company did the job with a four-truck motor flat car which had its own air-operated cranes. Elsewhere, the rails stuck out beyond the end of flat cars and at tight street-corner curves even overhung the curb lines. One day a long load couldn't make a turn without grazing a tree growing in the parkway. An ax borrowed from the lads at a nearby firehouse got the car crew off that corner!

In the Northwest, some interurbans had logging traffic in their early days. The Fraser Valley line of the British Columbia Electric Railway was one such. Similarly, a few logging companies not in the commercial transportation business used electric railway technology

Chapter 10 What Yo

The lading on gondolas, flats and other open-top cars was in sight to stimulate the imagination of every passer-by.

on their lines in the woods. As time went by, the log traffic increasingly travelled by truck.

On the Missoula Street Railway, finished lumber went on flat cars from a mill at Bonner (Mont.) to a lumberyard. Poles for transmission lines were common flat car loads, especially as they were needed by the railways for periodic renewals and by electric utility companies which were often under the same ownership.

Brightly painted new farm tractors and construction equipment were often seen on flat cars on Iowa interurbans. The John Deere plant at Waterloo loaded tractors via the Waterloo, Cedar Falls & Northern Railway (WCF&N). The largest shipper of the Charles City Western Railway was the Oliver Farm Equipment Company. Link-Belt at Cedar Rapids contributed loads to the Crandic Route (the Cedar Rapids & Iowa City Railway). During World War II, Dart trucks for the Army filled whole trains of flat cars out of Waterloo on the WCF&N.

An unusually large load was a 14-inch rifle for a battleship brought into the Mare Island Navy Yard at Vallejo (Calif.) on a four-truck flat car. This movement, railroad interchange, was completed via the Mare Island Freight Line, a joint operation of two interurbans: the Sacramento Northern and San Francisco, Napa & Calistoga railways. The Washington, Baltimore & Annapolis Electric Railway often handled heavy ordnance to and from the U. S. Army Tank School at Camp Meade (Md.).

Autos, "motor stages" (intercity buses) and classic Mack Bulldog trucks travelled past Chuckanut Mountain (Wash.) on flat cars of the Pacific Northwest Traction Company when the Pacific Highway was closed for repairs.

Circus trains only rarely appeared on interurban tracks, perhaps because circuses were accustomed to trucking through the streets from a line-haul railroad. In 1937 the Pacific Electric Railway brought Cole Brothers' train right onto Broadway in Pasadena (Calif.). It carried the show personnel and "not only passengers" but also the animals, wagons and equipment.

↑**What's in those crates? Charles City Western Railway locomotive #300 arrives at Charles City (Ia.) with a train from Marble Rock, August 18, 1949.** WILLIAM D. MIDDLETON

↓**A crawler crane is paying the freight as Waterloo, Cedar Falls & Northern Railroad #184 pauses at Center Point (Ia.) with northbound Cedar Rapids–Waterloo train 55 of August 19, 1949.** WILLIAM D. MIDDLETON

See Is What You Get

↑**With guidance from a man in the Georgia Railroad gondola, Chicago Surface Lines' electric crane #J203 deposits a load of rail at South Shops. The locomotive is #L201.** EDWARD FRANK, JR., ROY G. BENEDICT COLLECTION

Another visible commodity that traveled in substantial amounts was scrap metal in gondola cars. Probably all carloads were in interchange with the railroads.

In the days before air pollution was recognized, electric railways junked obsolete cars by first burning in open air. The remaining metal originated many a load which was shipped out via the nearest railroad interchange, often just a switching move. Removal of track from abandoned interurban lines, too, produced flat car loads of rail as well as scrap track hardware in any convenient type of car.

Bodies for Buicks were being made near Detroit in 1914. They went to the Flint (Mich.) assembly plant standing on end on flat cars of the Detroit United Railway. Covered with a large canvas, 18 bodies would fit on a car. The tarpaulin went back in a box under the empty car. Because of dependability, this traffic was

taken away from a direct railroad—although the interurban's rates were higher and trucking was required at both ends of the electric haul. Score one more for "just in time" delivery!

Setup (assembled) automobiles originally travelled to market on flat cars. However, that was not the only way they could go. The small autos of the 1920's often moved in box cars. They could be loaded through the side doors—with careful maneuvering. In 1948, Twin Coach railbuses which would replace interurban cars on the Houston North Shore Railway were brought to the Goose Creek (Tex.) shops in box cars behind the road's electric locomotives.

An *automobile car* on the steam roads was a large high-class (clean and tight) box car, usually with end doors as well as wide side doors, often used to transport furniture or other bulky but light freight as well as autos. Copying this plan, the Illinois Traction System in 1912 had two 60-foot automobile trailers in which even the end arch of the roof could be opened to accept high loads like stage scenery.

Bi-level and tri-level *auto racks* for long flat cars were developed in 1960–1961, after the electric railway industry was already decimated. However, the South Shore Line soon established a loading point near the Ford plant in Chicago for shipping autos this way.

↓**At Rex siding south of McKinney on July 4, 1948, Texas Electric Railway #950 appears ready to move off with a car of poles. Erie Railroad #7356 is 50 feet long, enough for this load; but material too long for one car can be handled with the ends overhanging empty flat cars used as *idlers* or by mounting the load on two cars.** WILLIAM C. JANSSEN

↑A jumble of scrap metal fills a 40-foot gondola being switched by Potomac Edison Company locomotive #4 in Hagerstown (Md.) on April 8, 1944. VITALY V. UZOFF

↓All will be modern in Chicago as soon as Marmon-Herrington trolley buses #570 and #571 are unloaded from their flat cars on April 15, 1952. ALLAN C. WILLIAMS

↑**Two poles against the wire, British Columbia Electric Railway locomotive #973 heads a train in New Westminster on June 25, 1944. The white disinfectant shows that the 17 pig pullmans have just been cleaned.** WILLIAM C. JANSSEN

Electric railways' traffic that was "not only passengers" included stock: beef cattle, sheep and hogs. The Eastern roads, of course, with their extensive street running, were not likely candidates for this cargo, but west of the Mississippi the electric lines handled stock just as the steam roads did, usually using the latter's *stock cars* in interchange moves with them.

The Washington & Old Dominion Railway had a cattle chute for handling cavalry horses to Fort Myer (Va.). The Fargo & Moorhead Street Railway brought livestock from nearby railroad stations to the North Dakota state fairgrounds in a flat car with slatted sides.

More significant was development of local traffic in stock over the interurban roads, particularly in Indiana where state government encouraged it. The principal interurbans in central Indiana owned a hundred stock cars similar in outline to those of the steam roads, but having interurban standards of couplers, trucks and safety appliances and restricted to use on the electric lines. Occasionally they also moved a few animals in box or express cars. This traffic developed because of World War I congestion on the steam railroads.

The interurban network directly reached the commercial stock yards in Indianapolis and in Louisville (Ky.) and also moved loads to rural feed sites. One of the latter was a carload of young calves recently turned out on green pasture after a winter on dry wheat. That affected their digestion as told in the words of passenger train motorman Wayne Trambarger:

"They'd have a train and a crew to bring a load of stock every so often out to Broad Ripple and then hook it on *us,* and then we'd bring it to Tipton and then take it wherever it went. . . . We had to *back up* to Funke's crossing (it's about three or four miles east of Tip-

11S

↑**Three Northern Pacific stock cars—including two old ones with wooden posts—have just come off a southbound Illinois Central train to the Charles City Western Railway at Charles City (Ia.), May 31, 1947.** GORDON E. LLOYD

ton) to unload that carload of calves, and [my conductor] had to ride the back end of it. Well, them cars had no bulkheads, and the wind would make his nose run. And he'd wipe his nose. . . . He had picked up all this green grass that had went through the cattle and he'd rubbed it in his nose and on his mouth and in his eyes and all over his face!"

When stock was moved to market, speed meant money. The interurbans advertised that they helped shippers "top the market—save weight and time" because stock lost weight while in transit. They were better adapted than the railroads to provide speed because they ran special trains direct from country points and, more subtly, because of what we would today call accountability of local management.

Over some routes a daily (except Sundays) stock train was scheduled on a less-than-car-load basis, accepting stock at loading ramps all along the route. Such handling did not even re-quire a side track as cooperation between the farmers and the train crews usually loaded the cars without delaying the typical hourly pas-senger service. But, one time: "They was three carloads of hogs. They were on around 200 to 225 pounds. They was the farmer and two of his boys and three of us crew. . . . There wasn't a hog that would go up that chute. We had to *carry* three carloads of hogs up that chute!"

Stock cars are practically extinct these days. Only a couple of hundred of them are still riding the rails. The reason is simple: In recent years the railroads have lost the livestock traffic to trucks. In normal times, that is. During a 1972 trucking strike, the rapid transit line in southern New Jersey had an offer of traffic to the soup plant at Camden. The farmer pro-posed to buy a ticket for each hog and walk them through the stations! Setting itself out only as a passenger carrier, the line was able to avoid this unique chore.

ves Weight and Time

←Among apple orchards in Washington state, the Yakima Valley Transportation Company has nine reefers for interchange with the railroads on this day in September 1945. W. C. WHITTAKER

←Bamberger Railroad #302 heads out of Salt Lake City (Utah), November 25, 1939. As it turns off First West Street into a short right-of-way it's only a block from the Temple. W. C. WHITTAKER

Interurbans originated *reefer* (refrigerator car) loads of produce and packing-house products such as dressed meat. Creameries sent butter to major markets. Onions, cabbages and potatoes were among commodities shipped from producing regions via many an interurban railway. Whole trains of reefers were found in major fruit-growing areas or on the Pacific Electric Railway when it met a banana boat at Wilmington (Calif.). A million bushels of potatoes a year originated on the Aroostook Valley Railroad. On-line warehouses permitted them to be stored for winter shipment. Imagine *Pacific* Fruit Express reefers being used in Maine to keep the cargo from getting too cold!

The interurbans also terminated refrigerator car shipments just as they did coal or cement or scrap. An occasional on-line food wholesaler received cars. International movements of perishables went into Vancouver over the British Columbia Electric Railway via Sumas (Wash.). Bananas, berries, cantaloupe, grapefruit, lettuce, oranges, rhubarb and watermelon travelled this route. In Rochester (N. Y.), produce sellers ordered cars spotted on subway team tracks and retailed their wares to the public right from the cars.

Shorter than many gondolas and weighing less than a loaded hopper, refrigerator cars gave the interurbans less trouble on their typically tight curves and light bridges. The higher-rated cargoes also produced more revenue.

Chapter 12

The distinctive yellow cars with the narrow doors carried perishables on both steam and electric railroads.

↑**British Columbia Hydro & Power Authority (as it was then) freight motor #960 switches a modern reefer at Carrall Street yard in Vancouver, July 22, 1968. At that time, this yard and the adjacent Canadian Pacific Railway interchange were isolated from the rest of B. C. Hydro and were the only electric part.** WILLIAM D. MIDDLETON

Reefers were owned by the major packers or by *car lines* rather than directly by the railroads. The car line was a corporate device of shippers, railroads or groups of railroads. The yellow or orange reefers, many emblazoned with colorful insignia of the packing companies, stood out from the dull red box cars and black hoppers then standard on the railroads. At least one electric sponsored a refrigerator car line: the Winona Refrigerator Car Corporation of the Winona Railroad in Indiana.

A few interurbans owned refrigerator cars for local use. The Illinois Traction System had nine short, light reefers resembling its traction box cars, but of course with narrow, heavily insulated doors hung on massive hinges. The Washington, Baltimore & Annapolis Electric Railway operated three refrigerator cars, obtained secondhand from a meat packer, for several years until 1923. The Texas Electric Railway and a few Ohio lines had traction box cars converted for cooling. Most of these were ice-cooled cars. The North Shore Line used five ammonia-refrigerated cars, quite remarkable when they were introduced in 1926. Occasionally one of them was seen on the rear of the afternoon merchandise despatch train between Chicago and Milwaukee until 1938.

Here Comes the Beef

Like refrigerator cars, tank cars were generally owned by car lines rather than by the railroads or interurbans. An unusual case was the Los Angeles Railway in 1902–1912, which used its own 1,844-gallon motorized tank car with an enclosed wooden body to bring oil from wells to its powerhouse.

In the interurban era, the majority of tank cars carried petroleum products. Typically they were moved in interchange with the railroads. From the oil fields, fortunately situated lines such as the Arkansas Valley Interurban at Valley Center (Kans.) in a 1929 boom carried crude oil and casing-head gasoline. The Sand Springs (Okla.) Railway served a Sinclair Oil Company refinery. Bulk oil and gasoline terminals were common on the remaining interurban lines after 1930. Not only were these products in demand for automotive use, but house heating by oil was the modern way.

Tank cars were used in "loose car railroading" just like box cars. But perhaps more than with any other specialized car type, tank cars appeared in solid trains on lines like the Pacific Electric Railway where traffic was concentrated at refineries, docks or pipeline terminals.

Water was hauled *to* the lake in a former Union Pacific steam locomotive tender via the Salt Lake, Garfield & Western Railway. Thus the Saltair Pavilion received its freshwater supply. Fourteen flat cars of the Pacific Electric Railway had big glass-lined tanks and carried Arrowhead Spring water from the mountains above San Bernardino to a bottling plant of the California Consolidated Water Company in Los Angeles. These two specialized operations were local moves. Molasses in trailer tank cars travelled over the streetcar lines of the Boston Elevated Railway from a refinery at East Cambridge (Mass.).

Several cities had water-purification plants served by street railways or by private electric lines built along with the plants, such as that of the Sewerage & Water Board of New Orleans. Distinctive "chlorine tank cars" (chlorine in cylinders laid in cradles on flat cars) plied these lines. Terminating here were loads of other chemicals and sand or gravel for filtration.

The increasing use of plastics is one reason for an increase in chemical traffic by rail in recent years. Liquid fertilizers for agricultural use also move by tank car.

Wheat had traditionally been moved from country elevators to flour mills by pouring it

↓**At Stop 21 on August 29, 1951, a London & Port Stanley Railway train climbs the hill out of Port Stanley (Ont.). Mostly tank car loads are hanging on the drawbar of locomotive #L-3. Too bad, the very next year a pipeline was built parallel to the railroad and the bulk oil traffic from the Lake Erie port was suddenly lost.** JOHN F. HUMISTON

Chapter 13 Tanks fo

Petroleum and chemical products were widely hauled by the electrics.

↑**The Charles City Western Railway provides some personalized railroading near Marble Rock (Ia.) on April 7, 1955. Getting the full service of locomotive #303 is UTLX #91990, an insulated tank car of the Union Tank Car Company.** WILLIAM D. MIDDLETON

(2,000 bushels to a 40-foot car) into box cars made more or less leakproof by wooden and paper *grain doors* in the doorways. For this seasonal traffic peaking at harvest time, car shortages were a perennial complaint. In the

↓**A vinegar tank car is being switched by The Milwaukee Electric Railway & Transport Company at West Junction on September 6, 1947.** GORDON E. LLOYD

late 1940's some railroads tried coal hoppers fitted with old box car roofs as an admitted makeshift. It was a good idea!

Cars were then built specifically to perform this service or to haul other foodstuffs. Some such *covered hopper cars* had the outline of an ordinary hopper car while others were round like a tank car. The grain load went up to 3,400 bushels per car. The cars could also carry non-food commodities in pelletized, granular or powdered form. Salt from an evaporating plant was interchanged from the Hutchinson (Kans.) & Northern Railway. Among the first of the new-style covered hoppers was a design for the General American Transportation Company in 1954. This equipment, owned by railroads or shippers, appeared on long-surviving electrics. Two leased cars carried the South Shore Line herald. A hundred covered hoppers carried the Iowa Terminal Railroad name in the 1980's, but they were used mainly on its non-electric Charles City Division.

Shipping by Trolley

←Let's start with a small, single-truck, home-built box motor. *Really* home-built—in the yard of Wells Elliott's home at North Hanson (Mass.)! The Brockton & Plymouth Street Railway fitted it with a truck and motors at the Plymouth carhouse. The photo was made near turnout 13, Kingston. O. R. CUMMINGS

LCL was typically moved in a *box motor*—a car of about the same size and power as an interurban passenger car but usually geared for lower speeds. A small interurban road with only a couple of passenger cars typically had a box motor, while big systems owned a few dozen. Box motors handled milk too, and on some lines express matter or newspapers, and they were versatile enough to haul freight cars or trailers. In early years, they often had folding wooden longitudinal benches for passengers during peaks on Sundays or county fair days.

To provide capacity for LCL beyond one car in a train, in New England and elsewhere box motors ran in multiple unit with their own kind. For this type of operation patent couplers

↓"Consolidated Electric Freight" motors bore the circle-P insignia of Pittsburgh Railways and the triangle of the West Penn Railways. West Penn made use of multiple-unit box motors by dividing two-car trains from downtown Pittsburgh at Hecla Junction. One car to Connellsville—the other to Brownsville! CHARLES A. BROWN COLLECTION

Chapter 14 Don

By whatever name, box motors or express motors carried much of the LCL and other traffic as well.

→Express motor #15 of the Millville (N. J.) Traction Company was obviously converted from a passenger car. STEPHEN D. MAGUIRE

↓Not much space for loading the freight in this narrow old city streetcar! Express motor #5648, seen on November 20, 1912, belongs to the Philadelphia Rapid Transit Company. PRT, HAROLD E. COX COLLECTION

such as the Tomlinson were often applied. They reduced slack action and could automatically make control and even air connections between cars without separate jumpers or hoses, but made it impossible to haul railroad cars with their customary *knuckle couplers*.

Freight service was quite impressive in the confines of city streets! The train produced a heavy rumble over the switch and crossing work at downtown intersections. When the motorman shut off the controller, the loud crack of the Westinghouse line switch echoed off the buildings.

Where municipalities frowned on freight operation but allowed express, managements called the cars *express motors*. This name seems to have been common especially in New England and in Ohio. Railroad roofs, not necessary for ventilation in these cars, and windows beyond the number needed for natural light made the cars resemble passenger cars. Don't call this car a freight car—call it anything that will meet with approval of the city!

Call It a Freight Car

↑Scranton & Binghamton Railroad "milk and express" car #53, a light double-truck wooden box motor with side windows. The J. G. Brill Company at Philadelphia built two in 1916 on this order. Despite its name, the line reached only to Montrose (Pa.)—never into New York state. BRILL, DUKE-MIDDLETON COLLECTION

↓**The carbuilder's interior view of the Scranton & Binghamton car.** BRILL, DUKE-MIDDLETON COLLECTION

With the usual economy of the interurbans, wooden carbodies were usual. However, a few lines boasted steel express motors. Since the cars were worked en route, it was a good thing to have multiple doors so that the crew could reach freight billed to way stations. Each side had one or two big sliding doors. Perhaps only the Michigan Railway had *three*-door box motors. In addition, small end doors were often provided so that long items like pipe in 22½-foot pieces could be maneuvered into the cars.

Lightweight, low-floor box motors, cheaper to operate, were often recommended in the 1920's but seldom obtained. The Kentucky Traction & Terminal Company operated two on its lines out of Lexington, and the new Texas Interurban Railway in 1923 used three, practically double-truck birneys.

In later years a car of a city company that looked like a box motor was often a *supply car* hauling company material like transfers which needed protection from the weather.

→**Often old passenger cars were made into box motors. Seen at Wrightsville (Pa.), York Railways #09 was created in the 1920's from a fine arch-window wooden coach, a Niles Car & Manufacturing Company product built in 1907 for a 6,600-volt AC line.** JOHN J. DENNEY JR.

↑Texas Electric Railway #506 gives little hint that it was closed in from the body of an interurban passenger car. Car shops of the larger companies could easily handle reconstruction work like that. Looks like a trucker has backed up too close to the handsome green side of the car at a loading or unloading point. WILLIAM C. JANSSEN

→Washington, Baltimore & Annapolis Electric Railway #3 shows the four trolley poles used because the line then operated on streetcar tracks with double trolley wires for positive and negative return.

↓An all-steel box motor, Indiana Railroad #715 stands at the Indianapolis freight yard. BLAIR FOULDS, NEW HAVEN RAILROAD HISTORICAL AND TECHNICAL SOCIETY COLLECTION

Box Trailers

Instead of running box motors in multiple, roads with large amounts of LCL could haul trains of units called *box trailers* or *express trailers* or just *freight trailers.* Similar in cross section to box motors, trailers were usually shorter, about 40 feet long, up to 50 feet in later models. They lacked self-contained power, trolley poles, control apparatus and even crew cabs. They were different from railroad box cars because they could turn sharp curves found in city street running. Architecture and finish were also more ornate.

A box motor could handle one box trailer, probably the most common train make-up, or in flat country up to nine or ten with a big loss in speed and agility. On some routes the competitive need to make long terminal-to-terminal runs overnight discouraged the use of more than two or three trailers in a train.

In Iowa and the "central states"—Indiana, Ohio and Michigan—box trailers were found on all but the smallest interurban railways. A few were converted from old passenger cars and a few were small, obsolete steam-road box cars modified to interurban standards, particularly radial couplers, but most had been built for the purpose. In 1928, 25 con-

necting roads in the latter three states owned 835 box trailers, some dating from the time when the roads were built, but many added in the mid-1920's. At that time the Central Electric Railway Master Mechanics' Association developed a more or less standard design, of which eight railways bought a total of 137 from the G. C. Kuhlman Company. Other builders produced at least fifty similar ones.

The steam railroads would not accept box trailers. The major exception was in 1929–1931 when the Nickel Plate switched motors and trailers of the Northern Ohio Power & Light Company to a 34-acre wholesale food terminal at Cleveland. The Northern Ohio then carried the fruit, meat and vegetables to points beyond its line via truck connections.

But trailers freely interchanged among interurbans, unlike motors which usually kept to their home road. Through trailers ran six nights a week between commercial centers on different railways, such as Muncie (Ind.) to the Cincinnati area. When trains traded trailers at a downtown wye in the junction city, it was literally a rude awakening for an unsuspecting hotel patron! Conductors' police whistles (used to signal motormen) shrilled, motors groaned and couplers clashed.

As late as the early 1930's such runs were filled by cars of different ownership almost every day, either the roads participating in the move or their connections. Cars of the smaller or more remote roads were less often seen, of course; yet cars based in South Bend (Ind.) regularly carried the painted message TRACTION FREIGHT—MOST DEPENDABLE throughout the state and Ohio and even to Erie (Pa.) via the chain of connecting lines. Trailers of the Indianapolis-Louisville line, Interstate Public Service Company, shouted INTER STATE in "box car letters" throughout the same territory. Some participants in interchange were less imaginative, or just didn't have money to paint their cars, but even so a freight train with cars in "box car red," maroon, orange, yellow, dark green, and even an occasional multicolor job proclaimed the various ownership of the cars.

↓**Milwaukee Electric car #M10—more functional than handsome.** TM, ROBERT W. WIETZKE COLLECTION

→Montreal & Southern Counties Railway's express car #503—at Granby (Qué.) station on July 14, 1948—is mounted on Standard C-60-P trucks suitable for passenger-train speeds. RAYMOND F. CORLEY

→Indiana, Columbus & Eastern Traction Company #875 typifies cars built for the Ohio Electric Railway. *Arch bar trucks* were usual on common box trailers. At Columbus (Ohio). M. D. MCCARTER COLLECTION

↓The central states' "standard" design was longer (42 feet inside) and had double-wide doors. Note the long shank of the *radial coupler,* pivoted at the left and supported nearer the knuckle. M. D. MCCARTER COLLECTION

↑**Constructing a wooden body on a simple steel underframe was within the capability of many a railway shop. Texas Transportation Company #1 is seen at San Antonio in November 1944.** WILLIAM C. JANSSEN

To haul a train of freight cars electrically, you need a locomotive: motors and brakes with suitable control, a place for a motorman, a way to pick up current, and couplers attached to the whole thing. It doesn't have to *look* like a steam engine, the only kind of railroad locomotive known when electric railways began.

↓**In 1940–1950, Walla Walla Valley Railway in Washington state was home to one of many Baldwin-Westinghouse box-cab locomotives. This one had been built in 1906.** BARNEY NEUBURGER COLLECTION VIA FRANK BUTTS

The place for the motorman could be a little wooden shack. *Cab-on-flat* locomotives of this plan were built by many railway shops. The crews who used them found plenty of names for them: "privy on a flat car" and others more affectionate!

The opposite extreme in design was to enclose the whole unit, giving the locomotive the shape of a short box motor though it was not intended to contain any freight. After trying one or two of these *box-cabs,* many a road found that they were difficult for switching. In back-and-forth service, the motorman was at the wrong end half the time and couldn't easily see where he was going.

One box-cab shows the versatility of electric locomotives. It had been built as a gasoline-electric, was changed to a straight-electric, and in 1957 became a diesel-electric!

Often preferred over box cabs was a smaller centrally located cab, big enough for the crew but small enough for all-around visibility from the control position. Rather than to obstruct the interior, the large, noisy blower (for force-ventilating the motors) and air compressor were placed outside. Usually they were in-

↓**Built in 1893, this four-wheel locomotive operated for decades at Joseph Cushing's flour mill in Fitchburg (Mass.). In 1992 it is at the National Museum of Transport in St. Louis County (Mo.).** NORTON D. CLARK

The locomotives that hauled freight trains were similar in purpose but different in appearance.

The smaller units by Alco–General Electric boasted gracefully rounded lines, certainly evident with the cream yellow paint job on Kansas City #1. TERENCE W. CASSIDY COLLECTION

stalled under sloping *hoods,* one at each end of the cab, which gave the locomotive the profile from the side of a church steeple (without spire), hence the name *steeple-cabs.*

With each axle driven by one motor, the minimum was a four-wheel, two-motor unit. In the early days of electric traction that seemed like a lot of power, so there were four-wheel electric locomotives on a few dozen roads.

But it became more common to use two swiveling trucks just as on passenger units after the 1890's. Four motors totaled anywhere from 140 to 1,000 horsepower depending on the motor model used. Yet the locomotive could get around tight turns, though not necessarily with cars attached. This format is designated B–B. Letters indicate the number of powered axles that do not swivel relative to one another

↓Some of the larger Alco-GE locomotives were more powerful—and looked it. Sacramento Northern Railway #654 frowns down on the photographer at 40th & Shafter in Oakland (Calif.). CATENARY PRODUCTIONS

ny Shapes and Sizes

←City Lines #2000, a Baldwin-Westinghouse Class B locomotive produced in 1917 for the Monongahela Valley Traction Company. The "city lines" are its successor, City Lines of West Virginia. The unit went on to other owners. Today (1992) it serves the Texas Transportation Company.

←Glendale & Montrose Railway #22 at Glendale (Calif.) is a Class B-1 locomotive, as you can see because there are no sloping hoods—only the rectangular sand boxes on the platforms. This unit wound up on the Yakima (Wash.) Valley Transportation Company. STEPHEN D. MAGUIRE

↓The New York, New Haven & Hartford Railroad was noted for its 11,000-volt AC mainline electrification. Its name was also on 600-volt DC power for the Manufacturer's Street Railway at New Haven (Conn.). Later this unit was used by Capital Transit Company, Washington (D. C.). NORTON D. CLARK

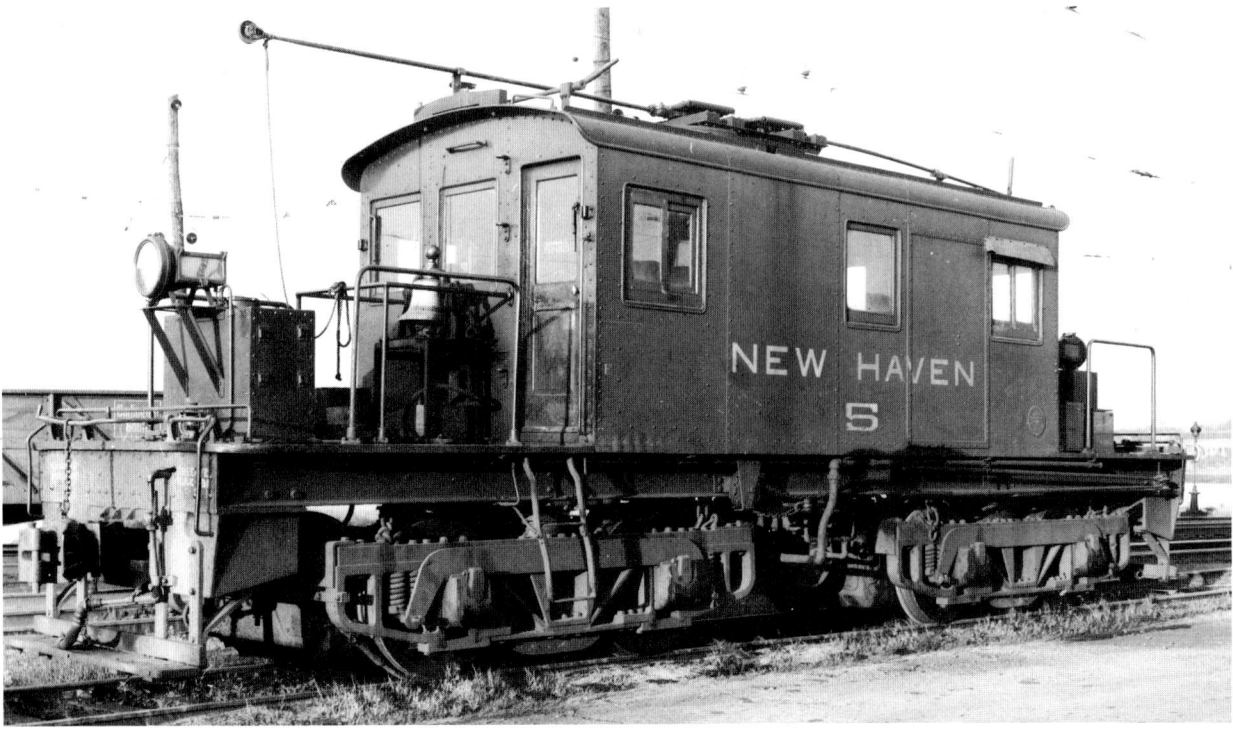

(B for two axles, C for three, etc.). The minus sign (−) indicates a point at which draft loads pass through the frame of the locomotive above the pivot points of the trucks.

Locomotives of this form could be fabricated of steel or wood by many railway shops. However, the commercial builders reacted to the market and produced lines of all-steel steeple-cabs. Alco-GE (American Locomotive Company and General Electric Company) teamed up to furnish one standard line, Alco doing the structural fabrication and GE providing the electrical equipment. Many of this group's output could be recognized by gracefully rounded lines and arched windows on the sides of the cab.

Vigorous competition was offered by Baldwin Locomotive Works, Westinghouse Electric & Manufacturing Company and Westinghouse Air Brake Company (1896–1954). They jointly produced over sixty of their *Class B* design in weights around 50 tons. About fifty more of similar architecture were as large as 100 tons. Baldwin-Westinghouse also sold a dozen of the 50-ton *Class B-1* with auxiliaries in the cab rather than under exterior hoods.

The frames of some locomotives proved unequal to the shocks of slack action. An alternative, workable on relatively straight railroads, was to mount the couplers to the trucks and also hinge one truck to another, relieving the superstructure of the stresses. This is an *articulated* (jointed) locomotive even though the body isn't jointed. A four-axle articulated is designated B+B.

Many four-axle locomotives were equipped to run in multiple units. They were often seen running in twos or threes. Hilly lines coupled on a pusher or two, separately controlling them as electric trainlines could not be run across common freight cars.

By about 1930, a handful of the largest interurban roads wanted more power in a single unit. This meant more motors, hence more axles. It also required a heavier unit lest it just spin its wheels. Dividing the weight among more axles made the locomotive adaptable to light interurban track and bridges. Most such locomotives had two-axle trucks so that they could take curves, spanned each pair of trucks with a subframe and mounted the main frame and cab across the two subframes. The result,

↓The trucks of this B+B articulated unit are joined at the center of the unit. The frame and cab ride above all longitudinal forces. GENERAL ELECTRIC COMPANY, NORTH JERSEY CHAPTER COLLECTION—NATIONAL RAILWAY HISTORICAL SOCIETY

↑ You can see that pulling and buffing forces pass through the kingpins, not directly between the trucks, of the Oregon Electric Railway's (B–B)–(B–B) power. Electrical equipment came from old passenger cars. WILLIAM C. JANSSEN

as exemplified by those on the Illinois Terminal Railroad: a (B–B)–(B–B) locomotive. This is articulation as usually recognized by casual observers. Ordinary street or interurban railways could hardly have accepted a larger unit, even if the amount of freight had required it. However, the South Shore Line had three famous 273-ton 2–D+D–2 locomotives 89 feet long. The numerals indicate the number of unpowered axles. These units were really mainline railroad power; other locomotives built in the same lot ran on the electrification of the Chicago, Milwaukee, St. Paul & Pacific Railroad.

The better locomotives were all but indestructible. As the owners went out of business, the locomotives went on to new owners, even across the continent. Locomotive 105, built by Baldwin-Westinghouse in May 1918 for the Auburn & Syracuse (N. Y.) Electric Railroad, may hold the record. Within ten years it had served on five railways and in 1960 went on to a sixth! One of the last sales of a used locomotive was made in 1980 to Edmonton Transit System. It had been built in 1912 for the Oregon Electric Railway and after 1946 worked on the British Columbia Electric Railway.

←On the South Shore Line, "big" locomotives replaced steeple-cabs. Seven units were reconstructed by this 1,500-volt DC road from 600-volt DC power of the New York Central Railroad. On July 16, 1955 master mechanic Merle Aldrich (left) shows off his men's handiwork to Daniel E. Ferner, superintendent of transportation. *His* men will soon be operating it! WILLIAM D. MIDDLETON

A Gallery of Oddities

→A three-power locomotive: trolley, battery and diesel. Illinois Terminal Railroad #61 (at Decatur shop on November 7, 1948) had been made at that very capable shop in 1939 from straight-electric box-cab locomotive #1559. WILLIAM C. JANSSEN

→Only electric, but three ways to pick up the juice: pantograph, sliding shoes on trolley poles or the insulated extension cord on the reel atop the hood at your right. Lakeside power station, Milwaukee, September 1940. JAMES P. SHUMAN

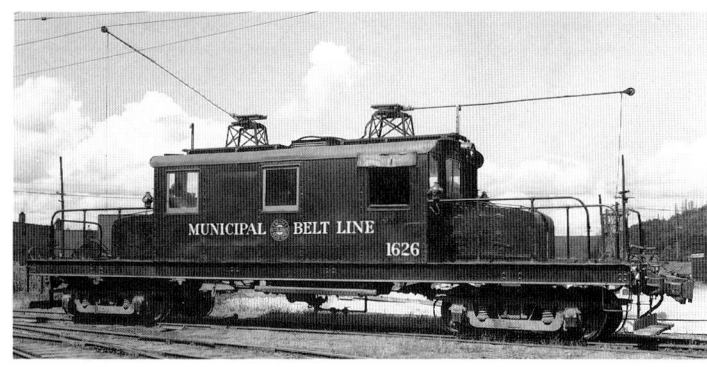

→Another very long steeple-cab, Tacoma (Wash.) Municipal Belt #1626. Short units often had all four axles equally spaced, perhaps equalizing weight on the track structure. This one tries to have half its weight almost in the next county!

→Hutchinson (Kans.) & Northern Railway #1 shows off its wheel centers because of its inside-frame trucks—unusual for a locomotive, though certainly common enough with PCC streetcars. ROBERT H. KENNEDY, ALLAN C. WILLIAMS COLLECTION

A caboose is a freight-train car which carries no loads and produces no revenue. Worse, it costs money to maintain and operate. Many interurban railways, especially those with short freight trains, found cabooses unnecessary. The entire crew rode in the locomotive. Recently many diesel railroads have adopted the idea.

Other interurbans, however, did use cabooses in trains of railroad-interchange cars. A caboose is often called an office for the conductor, but interurban conductors often found it better to ride the locomotive to stay in communication with the motorman. The caboose carried only a brakeman for rear-end chores such as closing switches behind the train when it cleared the main track for a passenger move.

←**Wisconsin Power & Light Company caboose #2000 (its** *only* **caboose, used around Sheboygan) featured trolley poles to feed lights in the car.** FRANK E. BUTTS COLLECTION

←**Southern Iowa Railway's four-wheel caboose #102 and locomotive #400 cross the Milwaukee Road on a steel bridge south of Trask, January 9, 1955.** W. F. ARMSTRONG

Chapter 16

A caboose was a freight-train car but brought in no revenue.

↑**Western Pacific Railroad cabooses sometimes appeared on the wholly owned Sacramento Northern Railway. This one dates back to 1910. Locomotive #660 is switching 40th & Shafter yard, Oakland (Calif.).** WILLIAM D. MIDDLETON

Traditionally the caboose was a place of a coal heating and cooking stove and kerosene lamps—even on electric railways with a more convenient fuel as near as the trolley wire. It would have been no great expense to equip cabooses with some elementary wiring, but tending the pole would have been an extra task, especially during switching maneuvers. However, a few lines had cabooses with trolley poles for supplying lights. Cabooses on the Chicago, Aurora & Elgin Railroad had electric lighting from the third rail via shoes on one truck, but they were in the dark in trolley wire territory. At least one line made a point of grounding the stove so that it would not be electrically charged if the smoke jack hit the trolley wire.

As on the railroads, most electric railway cabooses had bright red wooden bodies. Entry was by open platforms at either end. Seats in the cupolas provided a good view forward for observation along the train. Some roads in later years, as common box cars gradually increased in height, removed the cupolas. In the early 1940's the South Shore Line changed to steel bay-window cabooses.

To see a locomotive on the road with only a caboose—no revenue cars—was quite common. It might be on the way to pick up a substantial train. But, of course, on roads with sparse freight traffic, a train of a few cars may just have dwindled down to none in one direction or over portions of the road.

Revenue This Time

↑Car couplers are not automatic! The conductor and brakeman try to "lift the pin" to uncouple. View is from Indiana Railroad #787. WILLIAM A. STEVENTON

↑Brakemen spent part of their day on a narrow step. On June 25, 1950, Cedar Rapids & Iowa City Railway works at Cedar Rapids. WILLIAM D. MIDDLETON

Freight operation occupied fewer trainmen than the busy passenger service on most electric railways.

Typical interurbans carried little freight, so most train jobs were in the busy passenger service. That was the opposite of the situation on steam railroads. Some interurbans just called an extra crew when a freight load came in. To have four freight crews in a seniority district marked a "big" freight road. Usually freights were dispatched as extras, but they had more or less constant duties and calling times from day to day, so the men could pick the runs. Freight work was a refuge for the occasional motorman who didn't like wearing the brass buttons and dealing with the public but would otherwise be stuck with a one-man passenger car.

Steam railroad crews were five men: engineer, fireman, conductor and head and rear brakemen. Most electric roads' crews were four or less. A box motor, even with a couple of trailers, needed only a motorman and conductor. Three-man crews, the rule on some roads, provided more muscle for handling heavy LCL at way points. Railroading is heavy work!

While switching, except on the few roads that used diamond pantographs or third rail,

↑A universal scene—it could be anywhere that trolley freight was found. It is on the Indiana Railroad's last rail operation, between a coal mine and the railroad interchange near Terre Haute. WILLIAM A. STEVENTON

←It's September 1940. A minor derailment of a Union Pacific automobile car and a UTLX tank has blocked the Salt Lake & Utah Railroad in Jordan Narrows. Passengers are transferring from the car in the rear to #609 to complete their trip. JAMES P. SHUMAN

Oops!

The electric railways' freight trains could get into trouble in spectacular collisions, which were rare, or much more often by getting some wheels on the ground. Then it was extra trouble and many extra hours of work for everyone involved until the railroad was back to normal.

Even the few good men could have a bad day at times!

tending the trolley pole occupied one of the brakemen. You could push a trolley pole equipped with a wheel (less so with a sliding shoe), especially for short reverse moves if the trolley wire was tightly tensioned, but with no assurance that it would push into the correct track at a switch. Besides, how many freight roads had trolley wire in good shape? An unattended pole invited snagging on slack wire, bending the pole so that it would have to be changed out or even pulling down a span wire. This was a big limitation on two-man operation of freight trains.

7 A Few Good Men

↑The crew of Spokane, Coeur d'Alene & Palouse Railway freight locomotive #503 is ready to leave Spokane on this day in September 1940. But first they have to wait for a passenger train! Equipment is lettered for the Great Northern Railway, the interurban line's owner. JAMES P. SHUMAN

Interurban railways' fixed plant was designed for single cars or short passenger trains. Such a layout was less than ideal for hauling freight trains, especially with steam railroad cars.

Single cars or short hourly passenger trains spread out the electrical load. The current draw of occasional heavy freights, especially hauling upgrade, concentrated it at isolated times and places, taxing substations and the light distribution system. It is impossible to provide economically for intermittent peak loads like that. The first diesel on the Bamberger Railroad (Salt Lake City–Ogden, Utah) was necessary because World War II increases in freight traffic and through passenger movements were too much for the power system.

Often a train was hauled with both trolley poles on the wire to increase the current capacity at a point where resistance was high. Accelerating a heavy train at slow speeds could produce localized heating that crystallized the trolley wire or even "burned" it through.

Freights had to give way to passenger service. Most interurbans were single-track and ran hourly passenger trains, so the typical track saw two moves an hour all day long, plus additional Limiteds or suburban service at commuter hours. With this kind of scheduling obstacle in their way, crews might spend most of the work day waiting in side tracks for a chance at the main! If you work for a railroad, you've got to be good at waiting, and especially so with freight men on the interurbans.

Many roads concentrated freight traffic at night when few passenger moves occupied the tracks and drained the power. The Central California Traction Company, when it was an electric freight road, ran entirely between 10 PM and 6 AM to get a standby rate from the power company! How did the men get the trolley poles onto the wire on a moonless night? One locomotive was wired to turn on battery lights aimed up toward the wire whenever line voltage was lost. Elsewhere, placing trolley poles was just another annoyance in a night's work.

Just like steam locomotive engineers, freight motormen had to control slack action which could damage lading, batter the cars or even pull out draft gear. The "up hill and down dale" design of many interurbans was a real problem. Severe grades, or long gradual ones, threatened runaway cars. The Detroit United

Handling freight presented extra troubles because the fixed plant of many interurbans wasn't designed for it.

↑The tank car is out in front of the motive power because it's going into a facing spur in Richelieu (Qué.) after Montreal & Southern Counties Railway motor car #306 gets it to the south end of the seven-span Richelieu River bridge. In freight service, moves like this were just part of the day's work. View was made June 13, 1949. JOHN F. HUMISTON

Railway, certainly not in mountainous country, once wiped out a town bank with four runaway freight trailers. Despite an 8% grade, the Hagerstown & Frederick (Md.) Railway successfully handled railroad cars.

In freight service some cars must be placed from one end and some from the other depending on the track layout. In switching areas, or even for a few miles along the main track from the nearest *runaround,* locomotives pushed cars going into facing spurs. Other cars might be behind the locomotive at the same time. The caboose might be found anywhere in the train until the cars were rearranged for a line haul. The motormen ran blind, guided only by hand signals from brakemen. No hand-held radios!

At other times, crews resorted to a maneuver called by different names in different regions, such as *flying switch* or *Dutch drop* or others that are unprintable. It involved running a freight car by momentum into one track while the power scooted ahead into another. When successful, it showed skill and timing. When unsuccessful, it represented danger.

Interurban cars were narrow (about 8′8″) to fit closely spaced city tracks. Railroad cars by the 1920's were wider (up to 10′8″) and

couldn't pass passenger station platforms at car-floor height. The North Shore Line installed *gantlet* tracks opposite the platforms. Running on the gantlet got the freight trains far enough from the platform, but freights had to stop while the crews opened the switch into the gantlet and again to close it behind them. The Chicago, Aurora & Elgin handled the same

↓It's April 1946 and the head brakeman is out on the deck of Chicago, Aurora & Elgin Railroad locomotive 2001 flipping up the aprons at 5th Avenue, Maywood, one of twelve high platforms. All this to get three cars from an interchange in Chicago! WILLIAM C. JANSSEN

An Obstacle Course

problem by moving part of the platform. The edge nearest the track, a 2″ × 12″ plank, was mounted on hinges. The front brakeman used a pike pole to flip these aprons up onto the main platform. If he missed a section, that was a job for the carpenter gang! The rear brakeman clinging to the caboose steps put the aprons back into position. The South Shore Line's passenger cars were railroad width, but to handle super-wide loads this road had a gantlet track around a high platform.

Trolley wire was in the way where open-top cars were to be loaded or unloaded with overhead cranes. And some industries banned trolley wire from their private sidings. Sometimes trolley wire was installed to the side rather than directly above the track. A few roads had locomotives which could run for a while from on-board batteries. Several interurbans got their first taste of internal-combustion power when they bought a little gas or diesel unit for switching in restricted locations. A common practice was to use *reachers*: cars used only to span the distance between the power source and the car being placed or lifted.

Lightly built bridges and close lineside clearances required special care. By reducing sidesway and dynamic impact, slow speeds sometimes could ease loads past such obstacles. On a bad day in 1951 such care wasn't enough and a trestle collapsed under a Sacra-mento Northern Railway locomotive and 21 gondolas loaded with steel. New, taller steel box cars of the 1930's were too much for trolley wire clearance on lines not designed for any box cars at all. Imagine the electrical effect of a miscalculation! The Milwaukee Electric Railway & Light Company once had to spread a rubber tarpaulin over the roof of a box car while pulling it under a low overpass.

A few interurbans were powered by third rail rather than trolley wire. Low carbodies of some hopper or flat cars made these roads impassable for them. Several miles of track on the Chicago elevated had third rail for passenger trains but a gantlet with overhead trolley for the last of the coalyard trains.

Another whole set of obstacles came up where the interurbans entered city street running, as they almost all did. Small intermediate towns were not too much of a problem—the freight train just took over Main Street for a few minutes. But inching through vehicle traffic in the major cities required agility not easily achieved with the primitive air brakes of a heavy freight train. Besides, many municipal franchises restricted train operation as to length, frequency, hours or kind of equipment. As a result some roads used an extra motor car to "double" trailers to a siding at the edge of the city, making up longer trains there for movement over the country portion of the road.

↓No trolley wire in the Weber industrial district in Skokie (Ill.) on the Chicago North Shore & Milwaukee Railway, so locomotive #455, trolley poles hooked down, is doing its switching work on battery power. The batteries are under the sloping hoods. The North Shore Line had two such locomotives. LEE HASTMAN

↓Southern Iowa Railway locomotive #400 is getting power from the trolley wire with the side of the pole, not the wheel. Trolley poles are not insulated, except maybe by paint. At the haydite loader on the Appanoose branch, the wire was so far to the side of the track that the wheel wouldn't ride well. ED WOJTAS

↑**The motorman looks back because he wants to know about it if that flivver sideswipes his train. Just part of the trouble it took to get the Illinois Terminal Railroad's scheduled freight train 205 out of Danville.** WILLIAM C. JANSSEN

If the local streetcar company had built its track with standard grooved rail, the steam road cars rode along on their deeper wheel flanges. Their wide wheel treads overhung the railhead and beat down the street paving or got chipped off by high paving blocks. Street trackage used single-tongue switches rather than the split-point switches familiar on open track. The tongue was loaded with a spring toggle to hold it in position, but it was known to reverse under trains. Then a facing movement had better stop immediately!

Of course there were the curves at street corners. Track was rerouted across vacant lots, over by the far curb before swerving around a corner, or switching off to the left to reach a siding on the right—anything to get a curve of longer radius! The rare prosperous lines built freight belts around cities. The Texas Electric Railway got steam-road cars through Dallas by interchanging them to the Katy (the Missouri-Kansas-Texas Railroad), then collecting them back at the other end of town.

Railroad wheel contours gave trouble in sharp curves with grooved or guard rails because the large flanges rode at an angle to the rail. The extra friction sometimes stalled the train. Or the flanges climbed out of the groove and put the car on the pavement.

Single streetcars, or interurban trains with their radial couplers, could turn curves of 35-foot radius and up. Railroad cars can't! The limited swing of their couplers, enough for the straighter track of the railroads, meant that special methods were needed at difficult curves. The Illinois Terminal inserted extra hardware between coupled cars. Roads with only an occasional movement through town used less formal methods such as pulling the car through the curves by chain, not coupled at all.

The brakes might have to be disconnected as the brake rigging connecting body-mounted brake cylinders with the trucks allows for only a few degrees' truck swiveling. Patient tinkering could overcome this problem, but think of the trouble, hazard and expense!

The result: Many interurbans could freely handle steam railroad cars only on portions of the line, say between an interchange and the edge of the next big town. When offered an occasional car to other points the management's pleasure at the revenue it would bring was matched only by the crews' relief at finally turning the empty back to the railroad.

Not Only Passengers • 79

↑Many an interurban line had only a few passenger cars. Then came crowds on a special occasion like a county fair. Here on the Yakima Valley Transportation Company it may be the Washington State Fair. LE ROY O. KING COLLECTION

Box motors and locomotives were intended for the freight service, but interurban railways were versatile! These units were used as needed without regard to departmental boundaries. They hauled work trains on demand, and some doubled as line cars. They could pull passenger trains, either because of a temporary shortage of motor cars or, in later years, to accommodate railfans who wanted something "different" for chartered trains. A steeple-cab of the Oakland (Calif.) Traction Company pulled a passenger train carrying U. S. President William H. Taft into the city in 1911. Declining maintenance in later years saw disabled passenger

←The South Shore Line has brought the IC Boosters Club picnic to Hudson Lake (Ind.) in IC coaches. BARNEY NEUBURGER COLLECTION VIA ROY G. BENEDICT

Chapter 1

At one time or another, freight equipment found many other uses.

80 · *Not Only Passengers*

↑On Quebec Railway, Light & Power Company, the attraction was the shrine at Ste. Anne de Beaupré. Passengers throng to board a westbound train which will be routed over the Canadian National Railways. WILLIAM C. JANSSEN

motor cars hauled over the line by freight locomotives on some interurbans, such as the Salt Lake & Utah Railroad. There are even cases on record where a few paying passengers travelled in a locomotive cab because no fully functioning passenger car was available!

Some box motors were built with detachable snowplow noses. But whether or not so in-

tended from the first, a box motor was just what was needed during an unexpected snowstorm. It was powerful, not too fast and could be spared from revenue service for a while. If the road was in danger of being blockaded by a blizzard, freight could be suspended more readily than passenger service. Carbuilders promoted a combination box motor–snow sweep-

→February 15, 1959 is a less salubrious day. A freight motor of the Quebec Railway, Light & Power Company keeps the snow from drifting in on the interurban line. The site is near Rivière-aux-Chiens. OMER S. A. LAVALLÉE

Pressed into Service

↑This is no ordinary day in August 1913 in St. Albans (Vt.)—it's nothing less than the town's 150th anniversary! A newfangled automobile and box motor #21 of the St. Albans & Swanton Traction Company head the festivities.

er. But it wasn't practicable to mount the brooms when a storm came up, and they were in the way if left on all winter.

Special occasions such as parades saw four-wheel flat cars used as floats. The Aurora (Ill.), Elgin & Fox River Electric Company used a wrecked auto and bandaged dummy on a flat car for a safety campaign. In an advertising promotion, a 1936 Chevrolet was hauled through the streets of Portland (Me.) covered in a tight-fitting tarp so that you could guess at its streamlined styling.

↓A railfan excursion brought a remarkable lashup to Swanton (Ohio). The group enjoys Toledo & Indiana Railroad locomotives #80 and #75, express motor #54 and three cabooses. BARNEY NEUBURGER COLLECTION VIA ROY G. BENEDICT

↑At Waterbury on March 1, 1935, Connecticut Company express trailer #2037 displays an advertisement on its rear-end doors. If you were driving on a village street behind this message, would you agree that the trolley was fast? RICHARD L. WONSON

It Pays to Advertise

The broad flanks of a box motor were a good surface for advertising. What better place to attract public attention than at the head of a train? But lacking today's awareness of promotional techniques, or maybe just lacking money for flashy paint, surprisingly few interurban managers took advan-

↓Steeple-cab #82 of the Union Electric Railway has a shorter exhortation for you if you are a potential carload freight shipper in southeastern Kansas or northeastern Oklahoma. Plain and to the point . . . that was the Union Electric! ROBERT H. KENNEDY

↑Anyone who sees car #4 knows that Monongahela West Penn Public Service Company reaches a goodly number of places. Wheeling Traction Company was another West Virginia line that painted destinations on car sides. FRANK E. BUTTS COLLECTION

tage. The Grand Rapids, Grand Haven & Muskegon (Mich.) Railway painted wordy messages in block letters on car sides, across the windows and on the doors. In 1928 large multicolored signs on two express motors of the Texas Electric Railway, "Serving The Heart of Texas," urged the public to "Ride the INTERURBAN—Safe, Sure, Saving."

↓Many trolley companies presented patriotic advertising during World War II. Cars of the North Shore Line brought this red-white-and-blue display right to the Chicago Loop via the elevated tracks. BARNEY NEUBURGER COLLECTION VIA ROY G. BENEDICT

Railroading is an interdependent industry: relatively few carloads go from origin to destination on the rails of a single company. Because the electric railways were short, this was even more true for them than for the steam roads.

A railway that only occasionally received a car had simple interchange tracks, just a switch connecting with the steam line and enough space for a few cars to stand in clear of traffic on both roads. More was needed if the electric road developed much freight interchange. A second track, both of them connected to both lines, allowed separate tracks for receiving and delivering cars.

Each road was supposed to place cars from its end. One day at Mayville (N. Y.) the steam train crew kicked the cars too hard and they ran right through the switch onto the interurban main! Rather than report the incident and face discipline, while the interurban waited they added a few spikes to the rotten ties of the uncertain connecting track and ventured in with their locomotive to retrieve the wayward cars.

Lines with little freight might have only one interchange point with one railroad. Multiple interchanges gave shippers' traffic managers the competitive advantage of a choice of trunk line routes. The Joplin-Pittsburg Railroad interchanged directly with six railroads (five steam and one electric) at nine different towns in Missouri and Kansas. After World War II the Pacific Electric Railway was handling 3,000 cars daily through its 20-track interchange yard with the Santa Fe, Southern Pacific and Union Pacific railroads at Los Angeles.

For visual effect the accompanying photos show electric freights and their trunk line counterparts meeting at interchanges. Usually they didn't. Each carrier just left cars unattended on the interchange track until the other road came for them. Box car doors were not locked, only latched with metal *seals* which showed any tampering. Commerce is indeed based on trust.

A standing car earns no revenue. Besides, it costs a *per diem* payment to the car owner by the road on whose tracks it is standing at midnight. Alert managements of some interurbans ran an evening freight to get cars onto interchange tracks before midnight, thus making the per diem the receiving road's responsibility.

Freight cars could be interchanged by water. Chattanooga (Tenn.) Traction Company—an interurban—and some other electrics had docks where cars could roll from car ferries onto their tracks. The ferries had brought them from line-haul railroads across the river.

↓Sand Springs Railway locomotive #1002 interchanges at Tulsa (Okla.) on September 9, 1954. WILLIAM D. MIDDLETON

The points where electric railways interfaced with steam railroads were important places for their carload freight.

↑On July 29, 1963, Nickel Plate (New York, Chicago & St. Louis Railroad) Geep #490 shoves a cut of cars toward the South Shore Line interchange at Michigan City (Ind.). WILLIAM D. MIDDLETON

→Youngstown & Southern Railway (electric) and Pittsburgh, Lisbon & Western Railroad (steam) cooperated to move coal to Youngstown (Ohio) steel mills from the Ohio River. In 1952, 2-8-2 #23 backs up the main track while electric motors #101–102 back into the siding to pick up loaded hoppers at North Lima (Ohio). J. WILLIAM VIGRASS

20 At the Interchange

Freight cars and locomotives and train crews and tracks connected to the national railroad network are not all it takes to be in the freight business. Occupying public streets, electric lines had to get along with the cities. People along some streets resented freight trains, even asking courts to ban them. Such an action in Milwaukee closed a through interurban freight route from Kohler (Wis.) to Chicago.

By the early 1900's, legislation gave state *public service commissions* regulatory authority over services and rates. In 1907, the Hepburn Amendment to the Interstate Commerce Act placed interstate tariffs under the jurisdiction of the national regulatory body, the *Interstate Commerce Commission* (ICC). It would have put the big Brooklyn Rapid Transit Company under the ICC because part of the business was interstate freight carloads. Jurisdiction was avoided by handing the interline freight to the South Brooklyn Railway. A separate company (on paper), only it came under ICC supervision.

Similarly, in Canada the provinces had control except for railways declared by Parliament to be "for the general advantage of Canada" and those incorporated under Dominion legislation. These exceptions placed most intercity lines (including the British Columbia Electric Railway in 1929) under the *Dominion Board of Railway* (later *Transport) Commissioners*.

Each railway had to publish *tariffs* showing the rate which it would charge all shippers. Tariffs are detailed, complicated legal documents. They might include rates or special rules for individual *commodities*—to take an excerpt from the alphabetical index of one interurban freight tariff: "Hand baggage, Hydrogen gas, Iron sulphate, Lacquers, Lamps—electric, Lard substitutes . . ." Any competitor or shipper may take umbrage at any proposed rate and ask the commission to *suspend* it, making it unenforceable.

Do you want to be a railroad and deal with all that? What's more, if any of your rates are

P. S. C.—2 N. Y.—No. 49
Cancelling P. S. C. 2 N. Y.—No. 25

Only one supplement to this tariff will be in effect at any one time.

SOUTHERN NEW YORK POWER & RAILWAY CORPORATION

In Connection With

New York State Railways (Utica Lines) F-4---No. U-3

FIFTH ISSUE OF

Joint Freight Tariff No. A-3

(CANCELLING FOURTH ISSUE OF JOINT FREIGHT TARIFF NO. A-3)

OF

CLASS RATES APPLYING ON SHIPMENTS BETWEEN STATIONS ON THE SOUTHERN NEW YORK POWER & RAILWAY CORPORATION AS SHOWN ON PAGE NO. 4 OF THIS TARIFF AND STATIONS ON THE NEW YORK STATE RAILWAYS (Utica Lines) AS SHOWN ON PAGE 4 OF THIS TARIFF.

Governed, except as otherwise provided herein, by the Official Classification, (P. S. C.—2 N. Y.—O. C. No. 45, Issued and filed by R. N. Collyer, Agent,) supplements thereto and re-issues thereof.

Terminal Facilities, Transit Privileges, Etc.

The rates named herein apply from and to the tracks, stations or other receiving and delivery points on Railroads parties to this tariff, or to or from sidings connected with and operated by such Railroads where the particular traffic is usually received or delivered, subject, however, to such additional charges, if any, for switching, terminal service, storage, icing, car service or demurrage, diverting or reconsigning, and other charges or rules or regulations at points of origin, destination or enroute (as published in tariffs of the carriers parties to this issue), which may in anywise change, affect or determine any part of the aggregate of such rates or privileges or facilities granted or allowed, or deliveries made, as issued and filed with the Public Service Commission, Second District, State of New York.

The rates will also apply to or from stations and sidings of connecting lines, not parties to this tariff, at junction points with the originating or delivering lines as provided for in terminal tariffs of such lines filed with the Public Service Commission, Second District, State of New York.

This Tariff Applies on Traffic Moving Wholly Within the State of New York

ISSUED JANUARY 26, 1921.   EFFECTIVE FEBRUARY 26, 1921.

RECEIVED BY AGENT

Month	Day	Year

By E. D. CONKLIN,
General Freight and Passenger Agent,
Richfield Springs, N. Y.

↑The railways filed tariffs with agencies such as the **Public Service Commission for the Second District of the state of New York. Affecting only intrastate traffic, this tariff does not involve the ICC.** J. R. MC FARLANE

interline and were published by connecting lines, you must file *concurrences* agreeing to them. Then you must negotiate with your connections for the *divisions* which show the *percentages* of each through rate that will eventually be paid to your line. You may have to participate in *traffic bureaus* in your territory— for example, the *Western Trunk Line Committee* from the Indiana-Illinois state line and the Ohio and Mississippi rivers to the Rockies. The bureaus issued some tariffs and routings. They must charge you membership and participation fees. All of this before you get any traffic!

Chapter *21* What It

Railroading is more than transportation. It also requires meeting the demands of a regulated world.

COMMODITY RATES

The following list enumerates only such articles as are given specific rates. Articles not specified take class rates.

Item No.	ARTICLES AND RULES GOVERNING	Rate Applicable Between Any Two Specified Points
1	BICYCLES, not new, not boxed or crated and released....	50c Each
2	BREAD BASKETS, shipped full via this Line, returned empty to original point of shipment.....................	15c Each
3	BREAD or CAKE in baskets (per 100 pounds).................	Add 5c to First-Class
4	BREAD OR CAKE IN CARTONS (per 100 pounds)..........	Add 5c to Second Class
5	CARRIAGES, BABY, not new, empty or containing robes or blankets, not boxed or crated and released.................	50c Each
6	CORPSE IN CASKET, when securely inclosed in Rough Box, accompanied by certificate of transportation from Board of Health, Adults.......................... Child, twelve (12) years of age or under......................	$5.00 Each $2.50 Each
7	CRATES or CASES, berry or egg, in lots of three (3) or less, shipped full via this Line, returned empty to original point of shipment.....................	15c Each
8	ICE CREAM, in iced refrigerator carriers or packed with ice in open top tubs.....................	12c per gallon Minimum Charge of 50c each for packages containing less than 5 gallons.
9	MOTORCYCLES, not new, three-wheeled, not boxed or crated and released.......................... Two-wheeled, not boxed or crated and released........... Gasoline tanks must be emptied prior to delivery of property on Railroad Company's premises, and during period from October 1st to May 1st water tanks must be emptied before being tendered for transportation, and shipper must certify on shipping order and bill of lading that tanks have been emptied as above prescribed.	$3.00 Each $1.50 Each
10	SULKIES, knocked down...........................	$1.50 Each
11	TRUNKS, not new, empty or containing salesmen's hand sample cases, suit cases, telescopes or personal wearing apparel, accepted only when in good condition and securely fastened...........................	50c Each
12	TUBS, ice cream, containing ice cream cans, shipped full via this Line, returned empty to original point of shipment.......................... ESTIMATED WEIGHT, 40 pounds per 5-gallon tub. Gross weight to be used for all other sizes.	15c Each
13	VALISES, TRAVELING BAGS, TELESCOPES, SUIT CASES and SALESMEN'S HAND SAMPLE CASES, not new, containing personal wearing apparel, accepted only when in good condition and securely fastened	35c Each

7

↑**Specific commodity rates in the Rochester-Syracuse (N. Y.) interline tariff effective April 16, 1923. Every such rate could be vigorously defended or attacked by the affected shippers.** J. R. MCFARLANE

You may have to solicit traffic off-line. Even the little Clinton, Davenport & Muscatine (Ia.) Railway maintained an office in Kansas City. During the Depression such methods managed to get ten cars a day of overhead business—one-third of the line's freight. You must audit freight bills and settle interline accounts.

You must submit weekly, monthly and annual reports to the commissions. Unless exempted, your locomotives have to be examined under the ICC's ponderously titled "Rules and instructions for inspection and testing of locomotives propelled by power other than steam."

Do you suppose you'll need some office forces to take care of all this detail? To keep four trainmen busy the Charles City (Ia.) Western Railway in 1961 required a total workforce of 18 including five clerical staff. Oh yes, as to all your employees, if the ICC says you are a commercial railroad (not just an interurban) you have to comply with the Railway Labor Act and the Railroad Retirement Act. Whether it was subject to these laws was fought out in court by more than one company. Your general counsel (lawyer) will get some fees from you.

Railroading certainly is "not only passengers" *or* freight!

↑**Railway clerks had their hands, typewriters and rubber stamps full completing forms.** HAROLD E. COX

↓**Not to mention corrections to them!** FRED W. SCHNEIDER

kes to Be a Railroad

←**Tidewater Southern Railway in Modesto (Calif.). The 100 will be set out and steamer #132 will take the reefers to Stockton beyond the electrified line.** B. H. WARD

→**The trolley pole isn't helping Baldwin diesel-electric #1321 to pull the westbound Pacific Electric train in San Marino (Calif.) on October 7, 1950.** WILLIAM D. MIDDLETON

The contractors who built interurban roads brought in the motive power of the day: small steam locomotives, often castoffs from main line railroads. Interurbans that were converted from short-line railroads already had steam locomotives. Seeing a demand for interchange freight movement right from the start, a few roads kept steam until suitable electric units could be obtained, or even for years. The Southern New York Railway set some kind of a record by purchasing a secondhand steam locomotive from an industrial line in 1942.

In later years several Western interurbans rented steam power from connecting railroads, either temporarily during traffic peaks or regularly on nonelectrified portions of line. The St. Joseph Valley Traction Company in Indiana was regularly visited by steam-powered freight trains and gasoline passenger motors of its affiliate, the St. Joseph Valley Railway.

On the other hand, some large steam railroads had short isolated sections of electric trackage using conventional street railway technology. When you worked the Pasadena-Glendale (Calif.) local freight of the Union Pacific Railroad, until about 1941 you left your steam power at Arroyo Junction and picked up a steeple-cab electric for the trip through the streets of Glendale.

A few electric railways changed to internal combustion power for both passengers and freight. The Salt Lake, Garfield & Western Railway dieselized in 1951 but obtained a secondhand rail motor passenger car as well as hauling old interurban cars with its freight diesels. On a far greater number of lines, electricity was kept for both passengers and freight for as long as there were any rail passengers.

←**In East Hartford is Connecticut Company #2022, an electric express motor converted to include a gasoline-powered generator after the 1938 hurricane brought down elm trees and the trolley wire.**

The electric railways weren't and aren't entirely electric.

Some roads continued interchange freight after giving up passengers. Almost half of the Canadian interurban mileage was so preserved; in the U. S., a much smaller proportion. Of these, some made no new investment, keeping electric power and closing down when traffic thinned out or when renewals were needed.

Several lines dieselized all but short districts where municipal restrictions, sharp curves or light rail required electrics. Until 1965 the Sacramento Northern Railway kept an electric switcher at Yuba City (Calif.). Others dieselized entirely, mostly in the period 1944–1960, operating that way for a few years or even to the present. The 44-ton center-cab straight-diesel locomotive became the spiritual descendant of the straight-electric steeple-cab.

During the transition period, some of the big freight roads used both electric and diesel power in the same train. Each unit was controlled by its own motorman or engineer. On three lines which used trolley-operated wayside signals, diesel-electrics briefly sported trolley poles which only shunted the contactors on the wire, bringing no power into the locomotives.

Part of the Washington, Baltimore & Annapolis Electric Railway has had a checkered career since it switched its passengers to buses and de-electrified its freight in 1950. As the Baltimore & Annapolis Railroad, in 1961 it attempted suburban commuter service using a borrowed diesel car. Even freight ceased in 1972—but resumed in 1976 on 6 miles to Glen Burnie (Md.). Not only that, but the right-of-way is being adapted (not by the railway company) as a light rail line to open about 1993.

Numerous fragments of old interurban lines became short industrial spurs of big roads.

Perhaps twenty former interurbans still exist in 1992 as separate companies hauling freight. The longest such stretch of ex-interurban trackage is the former British Columbia Electric Railway line of the Southern Railway of British Columbia. The Cedar Rapids & Iowa City Railway expanded beyond its interurban heritage by buying ex–Milwaukee Road and Rock Island trackage and also by securing *haulage rights* all the way to Blue Island (Ill.)! By this means, cars under its control (on paper) move in trains of the Iowa Interstate Railroad.

In some cases the ex-interurban companies are wholly owned by big railroads. Sometimes two or more railroads bought a former interurban and kept its name, as with the Oakland (Calif.) Terminal Railroad, an offshoot of the Key System, which was sold to the Western Pacific and the Santa Fe. The Waterloo (Ia.) Railroad went through joint ownership by the Illinois Central and the Rock Island, sole ownership by the former's successor, the Illinois Central Gulf (ICG), and spin-off of ICG's Iowa lines to the Chicago Central & Pacific Railroad. That company still operates ex-interurban track at Cedar Rapids and Waterloo, but

↑Near Boone (Ia.), Extra 402 South of April 9, 1955 is a switch run from the Fraser power plant of the Fort Dodge, Des Moines & Southern Railway. In 1953–1962 the Fort Dodge Line bought ten General Electric diesels similar to this one as well as five smaller units. WILLIAM D. MIDDLETON

ICG kept the Waterloo's box cars and its name (reorganized in 1985 as the Waterloo Railway) and assigned it some former ICG trackage in Mississippi! Have you got all that?

The old interurban company names are gradually disappearing by merger into the owner company (as with the Piedmont & Northern Railway into the Seaboard Coast Line Railroad in 1969) or by abandonment. For example, in 1990 the 20-mile Visalia (Calif.) Electric Railroad shut down. The Portland (Ore.) Traction Company lost its last customer about the same time. Long line hauls of both the Sacramento Northern Railway and the Illinois Terminal Railroad were decimated by rerouting trains via trackage rights on the owner roads, a better economy than maintaining and upgrading the old interurban alignments.

Only one trolley road in the United States or Canada has been continuously electrically operated for freight service up to today (1992). The Texas Transportation Company has a mile of track—half street-running—at San Antonio. Its two locomotives bring grain and corn syrup into the plant of its owner, the Pearl Brewing Company, and take out loads of beer.

In 1992 the Iowa Traction Railroad still uses electricity to operate the line of the former Mason City & Clear Lake Railroad. While this road was the Iowa Terminal Railroad, electric operation was interrupted during 1967 due to a fire. However, with that brief exception the trolley wire has been used since 1897!

The railroad of the Municipality of East Troy (Wis.) had been a dieselized 7-mile vestige of the Milwaukee Electric for almost twenty years but retained trolley wire for trolley museum operation. Electricity came back for the commercial freight haulage of spring 1991 using one of the museum's locomotives.

The tracks of the San Diego (Calif.) Trolley, a "new start" light rail line, are visited by diesel freight trains of the San Diego & Imperial Valley Railroad.

In a dynamic national economy, industries and traffic patterns continually change. As shippers along the former interurbans change their ways, the remaining segments will surely dwindle. Inevitably the time will come when no sections of track remain in freight service to remind us that the electric railways once carried "not only passengers."

↑Electric in an October 3, 1974 photo and still electric in 1992 is the Texas Transportation Company at San Antonio. Motor #2 is doing the work. GARY G. ALLEN

↓Also electric in 1992 is the line at Mason City. It was the Iowa Terminal Railroad when this photo of Baldwin-Westinghouse #51 was taken. WENDELL J. DILLINGER

Part III Case Study

The electric interurban railroads in the state of New York were, for the most part, built to carry passengers from one large population center to another and bring the smaller intermediate towns and villages into closer contact with their larger neighbors. They were never intended to capture the through freight and express business from the nearby steam roads. The latter soon gave up the struggle for local passengers in the face of competition as the electrics offered more frequent and convenient service to the travelling public. The interurbans were also able to provide superior service moving local express, less-than-carload freight, mail and milk over their lines—so trolley freight was born in New York state!

In freight and express endeavors, the more successful electrics either cut across established lines of transportation or tapped territory not previously served by rail. Lines which closely paralleled existing steam railroads did not fare as well.

Some of the more visionary traction managers early saw the need to supplement passenger revenues by making concerted efforts to build up their express and less-than-carload freight business, both local and interline.

During World War I, trolley freight helped considerably to relieve congestion of local express and package freight on the steam roads. With this start, up through the mid-1920's the electric railways of New York state developed some interline trolley freight business, most notably between Syracuse and Buffalo. Trolley freight was only moderately successful, however, because gasoline engines, paved roads, ever-increasing operating costs and the Great Depression soon teamed up to bury the electric railway industry. By the early 1930's, two or three years into the depression, it was all over for most of the interurbans in New York state. Today, only a few traces of the vast network exist to remind the passerby that once upon a time small quantities of goods could be shipped by another way than highway.

↓**Railway Post Office car #3, seen in 1901, was made from a horse car body. Brooklyn Rapid Transit Company started with combination RPO-passenger cars but changed in 1899 to units like this one. It was manned by up to four postal clerks handling and sorting mail as well as the BRT motorman and conductor. ROBERT L. PRESBREY COLLECTION**

Chapter 23 Trolley Fre

In a typical region the electric railways involved the many types of freight service which we have described. New

This story of trolley freight in New York state begins in the New York City area, works its way up the Hudson River, across the midsection of the state to Buffalo, stopping along the way to pick up lines of interest in the extremities of the state and ending at the Chautauqua (pronounced "sha-TAW-kwa") Lake area in western New York just short of the Pennsylvania border. Practically any country trolley carried newspapers and packages on the front platforms of passenger cars or ran one round trip a day with its express car. The story is a review of the roads which, due to particular circumstances or aggressive managements, offered service beyond that level. Individual railroads are introduced by the operating names which they used in 1912.

New York City Area

Brooklyn Rapid Transit Company (BRT) served a city whose "wilds" were reached by long hauls on unpaved sandy streets—or by trolley. Streetcars carried mail from downtown to outlying post offices from 1894 until 1914, when the government substituted motor trucks. In 1896 LCL freight and express packages were added under a National Express Company contract. The draymen, seeing much of "their" business going to the trolleys, instituted a lawsuit. The court found for the BRT because its franchises specifically called for transportation of both passengers and goods. Later, American Express had the contract.

Bulk items moved by trolley to all corners of the growing borough. Building materials were especially common. Lumber, cement, sand, asphalt, sewer pipe, ice, marble for cemetery monuments and a host of other things went by trolley. Street sweepings, rubbish and ashes moved in gondola cars and in containers on trolley flat cars. There were 90 gondolas. Some of the rubbish was burned in the East New York steam heating plant. Who says turning garbage into energy is new?

↑Stone curbing and granite paving blocks followed new trolley lines in Brooklyn Rapid Transit freight cars like gondola #417. ROBERT L. PRESBREY COLLECTION

↑If you devised a car for ashes or trash, would you give it your name? Piper Dump Car #207 was patented by Col. A. R. Piper. ROBERT L. PRESBREY COLLECTION

↓The containers on BRT less-than-carload ash car #186 were the dumper bins of the era. All three photos were made in 1905. ROBERT L. PRESBREY COLLECTION

ht in New York State

Trolley Freight Railways in New York State

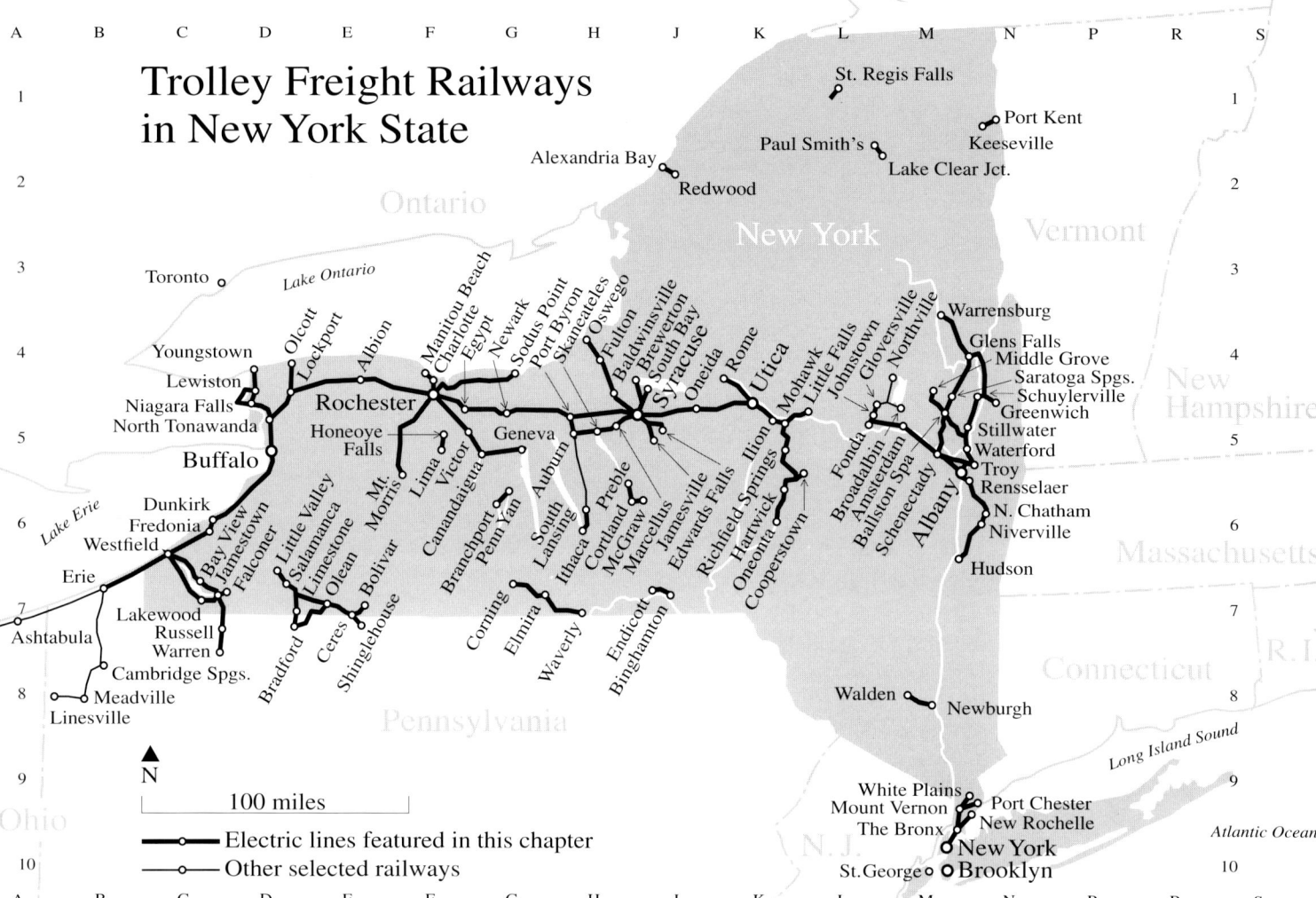

In 1900, BRT secured ownership of the *South Brooklyn Railway* (SBK), a steam line allied with both the Long Island Rail Road (LIRR) and the predecessor of today's West End subway line. Eventually the SBK reached from the Brooklyn waterfront at 38th Street to Coney Island. BRT took over its freight business on April 1, 1905, using surplus elevated steam locomotives woefully inadequate for the task. Fortunately, three small electric locomotives were soon in service. They and 40 freight cars put BRT solidly in interline freight business handling standard railroad cars. Eventually five more electrics were added.

About 1913, all of BRT's freight and express came into SBK to simplify bookkeeping and operation. By then, 60 to 75 carloads of freight were interchanged daily at the 38th Street carfloat and with the LIRR at Parkville (near 47th Street).

Construction of new rapid transit lines brought traffic in excavated earth and building materials. The SBK brought steel girders right to the abuilding Culver and West End elevated struc-

tures on standard railroad flat cars. The contractors building the Fourth Avenue subway in Brooklyn were persuaded to use SBK. Temporary trolley wire in the tunnel allowed trolley gondola and flat cars to carry ballast, ties and rail from a temporary track connection at 38th Street through the completed tunnel to the railhead. Trolleys were also used in grade-separating the Brighton and Sea Beach lines. They hauled excavated material away via the streetcar lines. Some was used to fill in the Coney Island meadows and the Flushing Meadow, later the site of two world's fairs.

Through World War I the SBK did a lively, profitable business. Later the convenience of motor trucks made inroads on all forms of freight traffic. LCL and package business deserted the trolleys so SBK concentrated on the dwindling carload traffic. Freight trolleys were scrapped or became work cars. In 1938, T rail in McDonald Avenue was replaced by deep-grooved girder rail. Excess trackage was removed, including many short sidings into former trolley freight customers'

→It's the 1958 "grape rush" on the South Brooklyn Railway. Every year Brooklynites of Italian origin bought cases of wine grapes by the carload for homemade Chianti or "Guinea Red." Normally operated at night, the street tracks on McDonald Avenue under the Culver el reverberated with Saturday afternoon trips to get the empties off the road. Locomotive #5 goes north with five refrigerator cars. KARL F. GROH

premises. Truly the golden age of the South Brooklyn Railway had passed into history.

To compete with truckers, in 1930 SBK received interchange carload freight and transloaded it to highway trailers of the Horstmann Trucking Corporation for delivery on or off its line. The cost of loading and unloading, which was absorbed in the rate, made this operation unprofitable.

During World War II, the SBK had all it could handle. In 1946, it entered the diesel age with two surplus U. S. Army locomotives. The electrics continued, outperforming the much newer diesels. Later better diesels were purchased.

Meanwhile SBK's ownership had seen some changes. In 1923, the *Brooklyn-Manhattan Transit Corporation* (BMT) succeeded the BRT. In 1940 the city of New York bought all rapid transit including the BMT and the freight business. Today SBK operates on its own track and on track of the *New York City Transit Authority* (NYCTA).

The last streetcar ran on McDonald Avenue on October 31, 1956 when NYCTA ended the Brooklyn streetcar system. It was decided in 1958 to drop electric operation due to the cost of rehabilitating the trolley wire and troughs under the el. On December 27, 1961 the overhead was de-energized. Thus the last bit of trolley wire left the Brooklyn scene. Some of the locomotives, restored for the NYCTA museum fleet, are on exhibit in the former Court Street subway station, itself a museum. The box-cab is at the Shore Line Trolley Museum at East Haven, Connecticut.

By the 1980's, about 90% of the traffic was received at Bush Junction (Second Avenue and 39th Street) with the rest from Conrail. The largest customer, NYCTA, receives material for track main-

tenance. In 1972–1973, 300 new R-44 subway cars were delivered to the Coney Island yard via Parkville. They made a trip *under* the Culver el before being placed in service *on* it.

Three small Brooklyn waterfront railways were partially electrified handlers of interchange freight, mostly interchanging with carfloats from New Jersey railheads. Largest of these, electric in 1905–1932 and operating a very minor passenger

↓To see a short railroad along the Atlantic Coast handling box cars of big roads west of Chicago is to understand the idea of interchange. SBK #5 works the Bush Terminal yard at 38th Street. STEPHEN L. MEYERS

car line, was the *Bush Terminal Railroad.* Its focus was a 200-acre industrial park of the 1903 era, where it interchanged with the South Brooklyn Railway. Each operating one steeple-cab electric were the *New York Dock Company* (1903–1908) and the *Delaware, Lackawanna & Western Railroad* at its Wallabout Basin terminal (1926–1942).

At St. George on Staten Island, the *American Dock Company* used an electric switch engine in its private warehouse yard until the late 1940's.

In 1901, the *Metropolitan Street Railway* of New York City contracted with a subsidiary, the Metropolitan Express Company, for express, freight and delivery service. The railway furnished cars and crews. The express company paid 20% of its gross earnings plus annual rentals for the cars (6% of their cost) and other facilities. On July 15, 1904, Metropolitan Express assigned the business to the American Express Company.

The service started with ten cable mail trailers converted for electricity. Brill later built new cars. All had plows for underground power pick-up in Manhattan and trolley poles for use elsewhere.

Six express offices were set up in Manhattan, two in the Bronx and three in lower Westchester County. The heaviest business was from the downtown station on Dey Street to suburban stations in Mt. Vernon and New Rochelle.

In 1907, a switch was built into Macy's department store. Cars ran to a Macy distributing station near the New York–Yonkers boundary. From there, Macy's made deliveries by wagon. Because the switch breached the curb in front of the store for private benefit, it was ruled illegal.

The *New York City Railway* (Metropolitan Street Railway's incarnation at the moment) ended the service effective March 15, 1908. The cars ran many more years in other capacities.

The *New York, Westchester & Boston Railway* was a high-class 29-mile double- and four-track electric railroad connecting the borough of Bronx in New York City with two sections of lower Westchester County. In 1913, its first full year of operation, nearly 2,000,000 passengers were carried, and by 1928 this figure had risen to over 10,100,000. Although "the Westchester" was planned and built for commuter service, it never excluded the handling of freight. The original equipment roster included one Baldwin-Westinghouse 80-ton steeple-cab electric locomotive, lat-

er numbered 701. Except on rare occasions, the one locomotive was sufficient to handle all the freight traffic ever originated or terminated on the Westchester. The Westchester freight trains, of ten or a dozen cars, were short compared to those seen on the parent New Haven. One wag was said to have described the Westchester freight service as one train going north in the fall with coal and another coming south in the spring with ashes.

Accounts of freight activities on the line are little known, but it is understood that all seven or eight industrial sidings were located between 180th Street, Bronx, and the White Plains terminal. The line between Columbus Avenue Junction in Mount Vernon and Port Chester on the New Haven Railroad's main line had none. The Westchester interchanged cars with the New Haven at West Farms Junction, just south of 180th Street station. The principal commodities handled were coal, ice, refrigerated goods, lumber and building materials. A daily switching service was offered.

Because the New York, Westchester & Boston Railway had no downtown terminal in New York City, it never developed to its full capacity. The Great Depression beginning in 1929 and the withdrawal of financial support by the New Haven Railroad spelled finish to the Westchester, and the last cars ran December 31, 1937, barely 25 years from day one.

Up the Hudson River

Between New York City and the city of Hudson, nine short electric lines extended a few miles back from the Hudson River.

Of these, only the *Orange County Traction Company* (OCT) appears to have operated any sort of trolley freight business. Opened June 1, 1895, its suburban division connected Newburgh on the Hudson River with Orange Lake Park and Walden on the Wallkill Valley Railway, 13 miles to the west. A half-mile spur was constructed to the Erie Railroad station in Newburgh to facilitate transfer of package freight with the steam road. The 1912 roster of equipment included two single-truck and one double-truck freight motor cars. American Express Company held a contract to operate over the OCT between Newburgh and Walden. In 1912, a modest 9% of the road's income was derived from package freight, milk and express. An early casualty of the internal combustion engine, all electric cars were discontinued by the end of October 1923.

↑Albany Southern's main freight house was within the city limits of the capital despite signs for "poultry supplies" and other agricultural needs. AS brought milk here for the Albany market, but even more was destined New York City via Rensselaer. On those shipments AS received 25% of the total freight charges. J. R. MCFARLANE COLLECTION

Capital District

The *Albany Southern Railroad* (AS) extended from Rensselaer (REN-se-ler), across the Hudson River from Albany, southward 36 miles to Hudson on the same river. About half of this interurban was a former steam road, the Kinderhook & Hudson Railway, opened in 1891. Eight years later, the *Albany & Hudson Railway & Power* took over the steam road, electrified it and constructed a 19-mile extension to Rensselaer, from where trackage rights brought the cars into the center of Albany. Electrification beyond the various city limits was by an unprotected third rail, one of the early side-running installations in the United States. Through service between Albany and Hudson was begun November 22, 1900. In 1903 the company became known as the *Albany & Hudson Railroad* and in 1909 as the AS.

Carload freight service was offered from the beginning, interchanging cars with the New York Central & Hudson River Railroad (as the New York Central was named until 1914) at both Rensselaer and Hudson and with the Boston & Albany Railroad (leased to the New York Central) at Niverville, about the mid-point of the AS. Motive power consisted of two locomotives, #L-1, a 46½-foot 50-ton box type from Taunton in 1903, and #L-2, a 40-ton GE steeple-cab built in 1913. Four express motors were used as locomotives from time to time. After the AS folded, locomotive #L-2 and express motor #27 saw service on the

Southern New York Railway. The latter car went on to become #320 on the Jamestown, Westfield & Northwestern Railroad in 1941.

Freight equipment on the AS included two cabooses, ten double-truck box cars and six gondola cars, all used in local service. The roster also included two standard electric express trailers.

American Express handled the package business on the AS but the interurban took care of its own LCL and carload business. There were no through freight rates with connecting steam railroads. The electric's local rate was added to the

↓Albany Southern locomotive #L-1 picks up a steam railroad milk car at North Chatham. Third rail of the main track is in view. WILLIAM REED GORDON COLLECTION

←Greenwich & Schuylerville's diminutive 25-foot locomotive #1 was available from day one for freight duties to the mills along the line between Stillwater and Greenwich. In those days people pronounced the town's name as GREEN-ITCH but today it's GREEN-witch. DAVID F. NESTLE COLLECTION

steam road's charge at point of interchange. The 1912 report of the New York Public Utilities Commission showed 62,766 tons of freight handled, the third greatest tonnage of any trolley freight line in the state. Nearly 22% of AS revenue that year was generated by hauling freight. Several industrial plants served only by AS were constructed prior to World War I. One freight train per day was scheduled over the road. It averaged 12 to 15 cars.

Eastern New York Utilities Corporation succeeded AS in October 1924, and the final day of the road's operation was December 21, 1929.

↓In 1901 locomotive #2 joined the one shown above. This conventional-looking unit came from J. M. Jones' Sons at West Troy (now Watervliet), New York, builder of most HV cars. WILLIAM C. JANSSEN COLLECTION

The 109-mile *Hudson Valley Railway* (HV) system connected Warrensburg on the north with Glens Falls, Saratoga Springs, Ballston Spa and Waterford on the south. Five miles of running rights over United Traction brought HV cars into the center of Troy.

One of the HV underliers, the *Greenwich & Schuylerville Electric Railway,* opened in the spring of 1900, was in fact a pioneer in trolley freight.

A 1905 landmark decision by the New York Supreme Court upheld an HV claim against the Delaware & Hudson Railroad that steam roads must interchange freight with trolley roads. Even so, franchise restrictions in Glens Falls and Saratoga prohibited carload freight trains in their streets so the freight potential of the HV was never fully realized. Coal, woodpulp and cement were the major products handled by two electric locomotives to a number of mills along the Hudson River at Hudson Falls, Fort Miller, Schuylerville (SKY-ler-vil) and Stillwater. Seven express or box motors provided regular express and package freight service across the system.

The company's best year for freight and express revenue was 1920—nearly $155,000 was earned. Income held up fairly well until after 1926 when the nosedive began. In 1928, earnings were about 20% of the 1920 figure. Final service on the HV was discontinued December 1, 1928.

↑A good load of passengers waits for the photographer and for switching of Fitchburg and Delaware & Hudson freight cars. Carloads to and from on-line mills and factories were interchanged with the latter road at Ballston. Ballston Terminal Company's #9, "A. N. Chandler," does the honors at Empire Mills. EDWARD BOND COLLECTION

The *Eastern New York Railroad* (ENY) was conceived and built primarily as an electric freight railroad. In 1898, it began as the *Ballston Terminal Company* (BT). It reached for 12 miles from Ballston Spa northwesterly along the Kayderosseras (KAY-dir-oss-er-oss) River through Milton and Rock City Falls to Middle Grove. By 1903, approximately 3 miles of sidings had been constructed to serve "twelve large manufacturing plants" located on the BT and powered by the river. Twenty cars of freight daily were claimed by 1903. Interchange was effected with the Delaware & Hudson Railroad at Ballston.

Reorganization as the ENY came in 1906. In 1912, the electric road reported 76% of its income from carload freight and another 3% from milk and express. That year it carried 103,400 tons of freight, the second heaviest trolley freight tonnage in the state.

In 1899, Jackson & Sharp outshopped BT #1, an early double-truck steeple-cab locomotive of modest dimensions. However, photographic evidence indicates that during most of the life of the road, combination passenger-baggage cars #9 and #10 did the freight hauling as well as accommodating the few passengers who chose to ride the line. Following a second reorganization as the

Kaydeross Railroad in 1918, the road continued its struggle for existence until the mills it served all turned to trucks. Last railroad service was offered on June 7, 1929.

The electric division of the *Fonda, Johnstown & Gloversville Railroad* (FJ&G) embraced 41 miles of line connecting the three cities named in the title with Amsterdam and Schenectady (ske-NEK-te-di) in the Mohawk River valley plus 13

↓In 1919 the Fonda, Johnstown & Gloversville Railroad electrified an old baggage car of the Delaware, Lackawanna & Western Railroad. The sun angle at Gloversville on September 6, 1936 emphasizes the flat end of box motor #53, certainly more typical of railroad than interurban car design. JOHN J. BOWMAN, JR.

←The Keeseville, Ausable Chasm & Lake Champlain Railroad shows off its train at the Keeseville station. Overhead trolley was used at both terminals, where third rail would not have been suitable. This photo was made from a postcard mailed on August 27, 1908. J. R. MC FARLANE COLLECTION

miles of assorted belt and local lines. The railroad's steam division consisted of one of the two rail lines between Fonda and Gloversville and the branches north of Gloversville to Broadalbin and Northville.

Trolley freight on the FJ&G was limited to five or six round trips per day of a baggage car between Fonda and Gloversville. The paralleling steam division handled all the freight business between the same two terminals. The electric division also operated a 35-ton steeple-cab locomotive, built in the company shop in 1903. It performed the necessary switching and freight moves on electrified tracks in the Gloversville area, usually short moves in interchange with the nearby steam division.

All electric service on the FJ&G ended June 28, 1938. In the 1970's that part of the railroad between Fonda and Broadalbin became part of the Delaware Otsego System and last operated in March 1984.

Northern New York

The *Keeseville, Ausable* (aw SAY-b'l) *Chasm & Lake Champlain Railroad* was built as a steam road from a connection with the Delaware & Hudson Railroad at Port Kent on the west shore of Lake Champlain westerly 5.6 miles to Keeseville. It was equipped with an overrunning third rail for a short time (March 1, 1906 to January 31, 1911). One heavy-duty electric express motor (#3) of unknown origin hauled trains including freight cars and the one passenger car (#2). In 1909, freight accounted for 37% of the road's income. Stockholder litigation caused discontinuance of the third rail operation and the line was completely abandoned in 1924.

Paul Smith's Electric Light & Power & Railroad Company, in the heart of the Adirondack Mountains, extended from Lake Clear Junction on the Adirondack Division of the New York Central to Paul Smith's Hotel, 7 miles. The road opened August 20, 1906. Its single motor car pushed standard Pullmans and freight cars to the hotel and pulled them back to the Junction. All provisions and materials for the hotel arrived by rail. Of particular interest was the railway's power system. Trolley voltage of 5,200 AC was converted to 600 volts DC for the traction motors by means of a motor-generator set in the south end of the car. Standard overhead trolley wire was offset from the track center line by several feet to accommodate a steam locomotive seldom used in logging operations. Electric operation was discontinued in 1928 and all service November 26, 1936.

↓A 50-foot Brill combination mail-baggage-passenger car, seating 24, powered substantially all car movements to Paul Smith's Hotel. ROY G. BENEDICT COLLECTION

↑A four-wheel electric locomotive of the Watson-Page Lumber Company. The trolley boards on the roof are almost obscured in this hand-colored postcard view, and no trolley pole can be seen, but some of the hardware for the overhead wire is visible. J. R. MC FARLANE COLLECTION

A rare breed was the electrified lumber railway of the *Watson-Page Lumber Company* in the northern Adirondack mountains about 27 miles northwest of Paul Smith's. Shrouded in mystery, the 4- or 5-mile line extended from St. Regis Falls on the New York & Ottawa line of the New York Central to a point on a river known as "outlet of Lake Ozonia." Running from 1901 to 1909, the line operated two small electric locomotives for hauling log cars to the St. Regis mills.

The *St. Lawrence International Electric Railroad & Land Company* was a 7.5-mile "toonerville trolley" connecting the town of Alexandria Bay on the St. Lawrence River with the New York Central at Redwood. One freight motor, two freight trailers and one combination passenger-express car hauled sufficient freight and express to account for nearly 22% of the line's $15,000 income in the year 1912. Service began August 18, 1902 and ground to a halt October 16, 1916, the victim of insufficient revenues and nil track maintenance.

Southern Tier

Street and suburban electric railway systems existed in several communities of New York state's "southern tier" of counties. Of these only the *Binghamton Railway* and the *Elmira, Corning & Waverly Railway* are known to have operated box motor express cars on a very limited basis. Revenues were of so little consequence that these services were given up about the time of World War I.

More extensive freight operation was found on one electric line along the Pennsylvania border. The *Western New York & Pennsylvania Traction Company* (after October 1921, *Olean, Bradford & Salamanca Railway*) was a 92-mile interurban system connecting Olean and Salamanca (N.Y.) with Bradford (Pa.). The line was located about 30 miles east of Jamestown (N.Y.).

The 1919 *Official Guide* stated: "Local express and baggage on all passenger cars. Fast and reliable freight service. Handles all standard steam road freight equipment except automobile and furniture cars. Daily merchandise cars from all points on Buffalo, Rochester & Pittsburgh RR. via Salamanca." The box motor made a daily milk run between Little Valley and Salamanca. It then handled LCL for Olean from the latter steam road's transfer shed at Salamanca. In Olean, one of the two tracks in State Street was taken out of regular service while the box motor made deliveries to the merchants.

The electric maintained track connections with steam roads: the Buffalo, Rochester & Pittsburgh at Salamanca and Limestone, the Pittsburg, Shawmut & Northern Railroad at Olean and Ceres, and the Pennsylvania Railroad at Olean, all in New York state.

Carload freight was handled by one freight box motor. The company also owned 25 gondola cars for an on-line gravel business and four box cars. Its cars were not interchangeable with the steam roads.

The system was completed in late 1908 and barely 19 years later, August 31, 1927, the last cars had run.

Central New York Short Lines

The *Cortland County Traction Company* operated a 16-mile system comprising a local line in Cortland and two suburban lines, one of them extending east to McGraw (5 miles) and the other north to Preble (10½ miles). The Preble route was strictly for passengers.

One of the chief reasons for the McGraw line was to provide a freight rail connection to the outside world for McGraw. Freight operation began in November 1895 when single-truck freight trailers were attached to passenger cars. By 1897 the traction was serving the local corset company, coal and lumber yards and a box company. That same year the Erie & Central New York Railway (later part of the Delaware, Lackawanna & Western) was constructed through McGraw so the electric's freight service was reduced to a switching operation, plus one or two round trips a day to Cortland with LCL freight, milk and the like for transfer to the Lehigh Valley.

All service of the Cortland County Traction system was discontinued on February 15, 1931.

The north-south–oriented *New York, Auburn & Lansing Railroad* (after April 1914, *Central New York Southern Railroad,* CNYS) was a 36-mile short line in central New York state connecting Auburn on the New York Central with Ithaca at the foot of Cayuga Lake. Originally it was intended as a third rail electric line. However, it was electrified only from the outskirts of Ithaca to the top of a steep grade at South Lansing (5½ miles) and then by overhead trolley. The company owned the Ithaca Street Railway system and was thus afforded a convenient 1½-mile entrance into the center of the city. For moving freight over the electrified portion, the company used a single-truck box motor (#1) and a home-built single-truck steeple-cab locomotive (#10). Early in 1913, Russell delivered a handsome 30-foot double-truck express motor (#11) complete with snow plows and standard couplers.

The principal customer on the line was the Remington power plant located just north of Ithaca city line. The Lehigh Valley Railroad set cars of coal on a nearby interchange track and the electric spotted the cars at the plant. Operation by the United States Railroad Administration during World War I kept the CNYS running, but traffic in its rural area did not develop. A proposed interchange with the Lackawanna never materialized.

The CNYS folded October 31, 1923, starved from lack of business. Traction switching at the power plant was continued by the Ithaca Street Railway until the power plant was closed July 29, 1930.

The *Lima-Honeoye Light & Railroad,* a 4.46-mile "toonerville," was an 1899 electrification of an abandoned steam railroad connecting Lima village with the New York Central at Honeoye (HUN-ee-oi) Falls. The property was located about 15 miles due south of Rochester and was operated in connection with a 200-customer local power company—really a case of the halt leading the blind.

One of the railway's two secondhand passenger cars was equipped to haul the few freight cars interchanged at Honeoye Falls. American Express operated over the line. In 1912, the company reported annual revenues of $111 from express, $961 from freight and total operating revenue of $4,667. Total operating expenses that year were $13,718. By February 1916, the struggle was over and the line was junked. Nevertheless, the Lima-Honeoye was a trolley freight line to the bitter end.

The *Penn Yan, Keuka Park & Branchport Railway* (after 1913, *Penn Yan & Lake Shore Railway)* was an 8½-mile line in the heart of the Finger Lakes section of New York connecting Branchport with the Northern Central Railroad (which was leased to the Pennsylvania Railroad) at Penn Yan. Both towns are on different arms of Keuka (KYEW-ka) Lake. The road opened for business on October 6, 1897.

Trolley freight was of major importance to this company from the very beginning. J. M. Jones' Sons of West Troy (N. Y.) built two double-truck freight motors for the line, #15 in 1897 and #19 in 1908. Both were suitably equipped to haul standard freight cars.

Inbound freight included coal for Keuka College near Penn Yan and supplies for several wineries and associated basket factories located on the line. Each fall, the wineries filled their sidings with carloads of wine in casks. In 1900, the company reported handling 1,000 cars of freight. In 1921, 57% of the trolley's revenues came from freight. For the first eight or ten years, Adams Express operated over the road. Passenger service ended March 13, 1927, but trolley freight continued until April 21, 1928.

→Short double-truck freight motor #6 of the Oneonta, Cooperstown & Richfield Springs is seen on May 7, 1904 with the Hartwick passenger platform at the right and the carbarn in the background. A fire destroyed this car and the barn on December 23, 1910. NORTON D. CLARK COLLECTION

Utica Area

The *Otsego* (ought-SEE-go) *& Herkimer Railroad* (O&H) was the most distant link in the chain of electric railways that at one time stretched from Illinois and Wisconsin to New York state.

Beginning at Oneonta (oh-nee-ON-ta) on the Susquehanna River, a predecessor company—the *Oneonta, Cooperstown & Richfield Springs Electric Railway*—completed 55 miles of road north to Mohawk in the Mohawk River valley. The first cars to Mohawk ran August 18, 1904 and within two months, the company had obtained running rights for its express cars over 13½ miles of the Utica & Mohawk Valley Railway into Utica.

The company was reorganized several times, first to *Oneonta & Mohawk Valley Railroad* in 1906 and two years later to O&H. July 1916 saw a name change to *Southern New York Power & Railway Company* and finally simply *Southern New York Railway* (SNY) in 1924 when the power and railway interests were separated by government decree.

Built through a prosperous farming country, the O&H did not parallel any of the established steam roads. Except for a tortuous five-mile-long 6% grade dropping down into Mohawk, the electric line was suitably laid out to handle standard freight equipment. Carload traffic was developed at an early date, and standard railroad cars were interchanged with the West Shore Railroad (owned by the New York Central) at Mohawk, the Lackawanna at Richfield Springs and the Delaware & Hudson at Oneonta. Through rates were published in tariffs and applied between all important markets on the steam roads.

Permanent and temporary side tracks were built and maintained by the railway company to accommodate farms and industries which would ship or receive goods. Stock pens were to be found at most stations in the early years. The company ran an educational program among farmers to show them the profits to be realized by growing vegetables for the New York City market. Grain, coal, hay and potatoes were the principal products hauled in the period around 1910. In 1912, 22% of the O&H revenues resulted from freight. Surviving records reveal that during the first ten months of 1927, 1,772 cars were interchanged at Oneonta, 773 at Richfield Springs and 79 at Mohawk.

→OC&RS locomotive #100 at the Hartwick barn. Other than steam construction locomotives, when built by Taunton in 1902 it was the first of a collection of electric, coal, oil, gasoline and diesel locomotives that would be used by the railroad over the decades. NORTON D. CLARK COLLECTION

↑**Southern New York Railway #80 tows Lackawanna and New York Central box cars at Index (the Cooperstown junction) on September 5, 1936. The company had acquired it secondhand only five years before.** JAMES P. SHUMAN

In addition, a lucrative mail, milk and express business was enjoyed. At first the United States Express and later Adams Express operated over the O&H until World War I. Joint rates for package freight were also developed with the connecting New York State Railways—Utica and Oneida lines to points as far west as Syracuse.

As passenger traffic faded from the scene in the middle 1920's, the SNY sought to bolster freight revenue by acquiring control of the Mohawk Lime Stone Company at Jordanville, 5 miles north of Richfield Springs. In 1928–1931, the company leased 50 box cars to generate per diem income from their use on steam roads.

Freight motive power on the property varied from time to time, the inventory being altered by wrecks, barn fires, etc. On the average there was at least one locomotive and three or four express motors in operation. The locomotives could haul about 15 loads over the road and one 20-ton box motor was capable of handling two or three loaded freight cars. In 1926, two handsome express motors (#214 and #215) arrived from the Buffalo & Lake Erie Traction Company and in 1931, the company purchased #80, a box motor, and #90, a 40-ton steeple-cab locomotive, from the Albany Southern Railroad.

Through freight motor cars to Utica were discontinued following establishment of a railway-owned trucking company in December 1930, and passenger service on the SNY ended July 1, 1933. Then passenger car #60, a beautiful 1909 wood combo built by Cincinnati and a real classic, was equipped with standard couplers and performed express and freight duty till the road was dieselized about 1939. The last section, 1½ miles at West Oneonta, ended operation in May 1970 and was torn up in 1971.

The 37-mile interurban division of the *Utica & Mohawk Valley Railway* was completed between Rome, Utica and Little Falls on April 29, 1903. In October 1912, the company was merged into the Rochester-based *New York State Railways* and became the Rome–Little Falls Division of its *Utica Lines.* The line was double-tracked for the most part, and as a busy passenger line it was protected by block signals. A track connection at Mohawk enabled Otsego & Herkimer (Southern New York Railway) freight motors to operate the 13½ miles into Utica where they shared the freight terminal with the New York State Railways—Oneida Line and Rome–Little Falls express cars.

The Utica terminal was the hub of express activities in the area. The facility had two tracks under cover with a total capacity of four 56-foot cars. Three classes of freight and express service were offered on the interurban. Rate "A" entitled the shipment to wagon pick-up and delivery at any terminal and certain intermediate points. Rate "B" included pick-up *or* delivery and "C" was rail transportation only. A charge of 10¢ per hundred pounds was made for each extra service rendered. A considerable amount of interline express business was handled between the three interurban routes entering Utica. In 1912, the 27,190 tons they hauled placed Utica & Mohawk Valley fifth among the freight-hauling trolleys in the state.

The only steam road interchange involving standard freight equipment on the Utica Lines was conducted at Ilion, 12 miles east of Utica in the Mohawk River valley, where the Remington Arms plants were served exclusively by the Rome–Little Falls interurban. A short double-truck box motor (#1996) converted from a snow plow switched steam road cars between the plant and a nearby interchange with the West Shore Railroad of the New York Central. This electric service generated an annual revenue in excess of $5,000 even in the late 1920's.

On June 15, 1907, the *Oneida Railway* began operating a high-speed interurban service over the electrified double, three and four-track main line of the West Shore Railroad between Syracuse and Utica, 48½ miles. After October 1912 this operation was the *New York State Railways—Oneida Line*. The West Shore, otherwise a steam railroad, was owned by and leased to the New York Central & Hudson River Railroad (after 1914, the New York Central Railroad).

Current was collected from an underrunning third rail patterned after New York Central's Grand Central Terminal installation in New York City. Limited passenger cars making two intermediate stops ran from terminal to terminal in 1 hour and 28 minutes, the 28 minutes being consumed in street running at each end of the 43-mile third rail section. Local cars left the West Shore at the edge of the city of Oneida (oh-NY-da), about midway of the road, and after passing through that city's streets, re-entered the third rail territory at the other end of town. The New York Central continued to provide local carload freight service by steam locomotives but the Oneida Line operated a package express car over the line twice a day except Sunday. Rolling stock began and ended with two 56-foot Brill express motors (#406 and #408) supplemented by #404 transferred from the Rome–Little Falls line.

The Oneida Line express cars operated from the Syracuse express terminal of the Auburn & Syracuse on West Fayette Street. It was located a mile or so from the Belden Avenue facility which served the interurbans operating north and west from Syracuse. Interline movements of trolley freight through Syracuse were virtually nil. For reasons unknown, such traffic never developed so a union terminal was not required.

Local express traffic on the Oneida Line was handled on the same basis as on the Rome–Little Falls line. "A," "B" and "C" classes of service were offered. For a time prior to World War I, National Express is understood to have operated over the interurban between Syracuse and Utica. The express or package freight business held up sufficiently throughout the life of the Oneida Line to warrant the same double-daily schedule until the line was discontinued December 31, 1930.

Syracuse Area

The *Syracuse & Suburban Railroad* (after April 1923, *Syracuse & Eastern Railroad*) was a single-track roadside trolley built eastward from Syracuse to Fayetteville, Manlius and Edwards Falls, 11½ miles. The road opened July 16, 1898. A 4-mile branch connected Jamesville with the main line at DeWitt, 5 miles east of Syracuse.

A modest package express business was carried on with one double-truck express motor. The company shared a freight terminal in Syracuse with the Auburn & Syracuse and New York State Railways—Oneida Line cars but no joint express tariffs existed. Except for an occasional volume move of stone ballast from Jamesville quarry to the New York State Railways—Syracuse Lines, revenues from freight and express were meager. All service on the "Suburban" ceased October 24, 1931.

On August 27, 1908, the *Syracuse & South Bay Electric Railroad* (after May 1917, *Syracuse Northern Electric Railway*) opened a double-track electric railway northerly from Syracuse City Line to South Bay on Oneida Lake, 10 miles.

↓An Oneida Railway "electric express" motor, by now lettered for New York State Railways, exchanges cargo with a company wagon. JAMES I. BARSTOW COLLECTION

↑The Oswego interurban line reached out gradually from Syracuse, opening in stages in 1899–1911. Syracuse, Lake Shore & Northern express motor #42 stands in front of the Clark Building on 1st Street soon after Fulton (N. Y.) became the end of the track in 1909. JAMES I. BARSTOW COLLECTION VIA J. R. MC FARLANE

Trackage rights brought the interurban 2½ miles into the center of Syracuse. On November 2, 1912 a 6-mile branch was opened from a point north of North Syracuse to Brewerton at the west end of Oneida Lake.

The "Bay Road" was designed to handle carload freight because there was no other railroad in North Syracuse. An interchange with the New York Central was located at Syracuse City Line. This interchange was actually an electrified extension of the steam road's industrial siding into Crouse-Hinds Company, well-known manufacturer of electrical fixtures including headlights for traction cars. Coal and lumber were among the northbound products moved to sidings in North Syracuse. Ice from Oneida Lake was moved to Syracuse in the early days. Twice-daily local express trips were made over the road from the Syracuse electric freight terminal used jointly with the Oswego and Rochester interurbans. The "Bay Road" was the last interurban to operate out of Syracuse, expiring January 11, 1932.

Syracuse, Lake Shore & Northern Railroad was a high-speed interurban running north from Syracuse to Oswego (oss-WEE-go) on Lake On-

tario, 38½ miles. From 1913 to 1917 it was part of *Empire United Railways,* and after August 1917 it became the *Empire State Railroad.* It was all on private right-of-way except through three intermediate towns. The first 14 miles north to Baldwinsville was double-tracked and the balance was single track. The entire line was protected by block signals. The road was completed to Oswego on July 26, 1911.

Until the mid-1920's, there was sufficient local package freight and express business to warrant two round-trip express motors a day. Connections were made at the Syracuse freight terminal with cars of the Rochester & Syracuse line and the South Bay road. As the 1920's wore on, the Empire State Railroad service was reduced as demand decreased. The Syracuse-Oswego cars stopped running June 24, 1931.

The *Rochester, Syracuse & Eastern Railroad* (RS&E) completed its 87-mile double-track high-speed electric line between Rochester and Syracuse December 18, 1909. This interurban railroad was built entirely on private right-of-way except through portions of eight intermediate towns. Cars operated over the Rochester City Lines of

↑A Rochester, Syracuse & Eastern express car transacts business at Warners (N. Y.), 10 miles west of Syracuse. These "chalets" were found along all "Beebe System" lines from Syracuse to Rochester, Auburn, Oswego and South Bay. Built of chestnut, they were more elaborate than shelters on most interurbans. FRED W. SCHNEIDER III COLLECTION

New York State Railways and for the last five miles into Syracuse over the tracks of the Syracuse, Lake Shore & Northern Railroad. Like the latter road, the RS&E was part of the *Empire United Railways* from 1913 to 1917. In September of that year it emerged as the *Rochester & Syracuse Railroad.*

The RS&E and the Buffalo, Lockport & Rochester Railway shared space in the Erie Railroad's Rochester freight house even though in the early years there was no through movement of trolley freight. The Syracuse freight house on Belden Avenue was a joint operation with the Oswego and South Bay interurbans. At eight intermediate stations, the RS&E maintained handsome combination passenger and freight stations. Each 20′ × 50′ freight room provided for wagon delivery on one side and had a one- or two-car siding for express cars on the other.

A double-daily local package freight and express service was offered using a pair of 68,000-pound Niles express motors. Three additional similar cars were purchased from Kuhlman in 1914. The RS&E and associated roads advertised USE OUR HIGH SPEED ELECTRIC FREIGHT SERVICE AT SLOW FREIGHT RATES. LCL freight and express rates were comparable with the neighboring New York Central but the interurban service was superior.

September 1911 saw the beginning of Wells Fargo express operation over the RS&E. This service lasted into 1918, when the old-line express companies merged into American Railway Express and the interurban runs were cast aside for the more lucrative steam road operations.

In season, fresh vegetables were hauled to a cannery at Egypt (14 miles east of Rochester), the only industrial siding on the RS&E. For a time, one of the express cars was equipped with meat hooks during a period when calves were being shipped to Rochester. Store-door delivery by local trucking firms from the Syracuse and Rochester terminals was inaugurated in 1925. This feature was not particularly successful.

The RS&E was not designed to handle carload freight in interchange from the steam roads since the interurban closely paralleled two lines of the New York Central: the four-track main line and the double-track West Shore Division. Carloads of coal for the Newark car shops were handled from the West Shore interchange track east of Newark but two curves of only 75-foot radius in the streets of Newark made the job difficult.

↑**Rochester & Syracuse #61 at New York State Railways' Rochester freight house in 1926. This terminal, new in 1921, was reached by running through the company's State Street barn–office building.** J. R. MC FARLANE COLLECTION

Local freight revenues held up fairly well through the 1920's. As late as 1927, over 17% of the company's revenue was derived from freight and of that, over 80% was local. Nevertheless, a receiver arrived on the property soon after the onslaught of the Great Depression and all service ended June 27, 1931.

Opened June 28, 1908, the *Auburn & Northern Electric Railroad* (A&N) was part of *Empire United Railways,* 1913–1917, and *Empire State Railroad* after August 1917. The A&N was a 9-mile roadside electric line connecting Auburn with the main line of the interurban Rochester, Syracuse & Eastern Railroad (RS&E) at Port Byron, 26 miles west of Syracuse and 61 miles east of Rochester. The A&N operation was tied closely to the RS&E to the extent that tariffs of the latter line indicated Auburn as an on-line station. Local freight traffic on the A&N was nil. The express runs shown in the timetables were in many cases side trips of the RS&E or later Rochester & Syracuse (R&S) cars. Service on the A&N was maintained until June 27, 1931, the day the R&S stopped running.

The *Auburn & Syracuse Electric Railroad* (A&S) was one of the oldest interurbans in the Syracuse area. The 27-mile line was opened from Auburn to Syracuse on June 23, 1903. The westerly 8 miles was a single-track roadside operation,

but east of Skaneateles (scan-ee-AT-luss), a well-graded double track on private right-of-way prevailed. Trackage rights over New York State Railways were necessary to bring A&S cars 3 miles into the center of Syracuse. In Auburn, a freight station was shared with the Auburn & Northern, and in Syracuse the A&S freight house had Oneida Line and Syracuse & Suburban cars as tenants.

The usual express motor cars plied the road twice daily. In addition, the A&S had one very prosperous industry on its line, Semet-Solvay (later Solvay Process Company), which operated a stone quarry at Split Rock, 6 miles west of Syracuse. Carload lots of coal were received in interchange from the Marcellus & Otisco Lake Railway at Marcellus, 12½ miles west of Syracuse. The A&S line car could manage two coal cars per trip over the hilly terrain to the quarry.

During World War I, the A&S bought a 50-ton Baldwin-Westinghouse steeple-cab electric locomotive to handle the increased freight business to and from the quarry, but kept it for only a year. A published tariff of the period provided for a flat charge of $15 per loaded car regardless of weight or contents. When moved in multiples of two cars, the second car cost only $14. After the war, the quarry was closed and the locomotive sold. It has survived many decades, however, through sale to lines in Ontario, and is presently on the roster of the Connecticut Electric Railway trolley museum at Warehouse Point, Connecticut.

2282-A

EMPIRE UNITED RAILWAYS

NO. 3 TIME SHOWN IS LEAVING TIME

EFFECTIVE SEPTEMBER 25, 1916

EMPIRE UNITED RAILWAYS

TIME TABLE

EMPIRE UNITED RAILWAYS, INC.

Rochester, Syracuse & Eastern R. R. Co.   Syracuse, Lakeshore & Northern R. R. Co.

Fast and Frequent Electric Freight Service

BETWEEN

Adams Basin	Eagle Harbor	Knowlesville	Middleport	Port Byron	Warner
Albion	Fairport	Lyons	Memphis	Rochester	Weedsport
Auburn	Fulton	Lockport	Newark	Savannah	
Baldwinsville	Gasport	Macedon	Oswego	Skaneateles	
Brockport	Holley	Marcellus	Palmyra	Syracuse	
Clyde	Hulberton	Medina	Phoenix	Spencerport	
East Rochester	Jordan	Minetto	Port Gibson	Split Rock	

Also Marion via Newark and Cato, Ira, Martville, Sterling, Fair Haven and North Fair Haven via Weedsport

Rates Between Above Points Are Strictly Competitive with the Slower Steam Routes

EASTBOUND	*300	302-306	304-308	310
Lv. Rochester	10.30 P.M.	12.15 A.M.	2.00 A.M.	12.00 P.M.
" E. Blvd. Road	11.00 "	12.45 "	2.15 "	12.30 "
" E. Rochester	.....	.....	.....	12.40 "
" Fairport	.....	.....	2.50 "	1.00 "
" Egypt	.....	.....	.....	1.06 "
" Macedon	.....	.....	.....	1.20 "
" Palmyra	.....	.....	3.45 "	1.40 "
" Port Gibson	.....	.....	3.53 "	1.48 "
Ar. Newark	.....	1.39 A.M.	4.02 "	2.00 "
Lv. Newark	.....	6.10 A.M.	1.40 P.M.	2.20 "
" Lyons	.....	6.30 "	2.05 "	2.40 "
" Locke Berlin	.....	6.35 "	2.11 "	2.47 "
" Clyde	.....	7.15 "	2.45 "	3.05 "
" Savannah	.....	7.45 "	2.55 "	3.20 "
" Montezuma	.....	7.52 "	3.02 "	3.27 "
Ar. Port Byron	12.38 A.M.	8.00 "	3.10 "	3.35 "
Lv. Port Byron	.....	8.00 A.M.	4.00 P.M.	4.00 "
Ar. Auburn	.....	8.25 "	4.25 "	4.25 "
Lv. Auburn	.....	9.15 A.M.	.....	5.35 "
Ar. Port Byron	.....	9.37 "	.....	6.00 "
Lv. Port Byron	12.52 A.M.	10.05 A.M.	3.15 P.M.	
" Weedsport	1.13 "	10.15 "	3.25 "	
" Jordan	1.36 "	10.30 "	3.40 "	
" Memphis	1.43 "	10.37 "	3.47 "	
" Warner	1.48 "	10.42 "	3.52 "	
Ar. Syracuse	2.13 "	11.05 "	4.15 "	

WESTBOUND	301	303	305	307
Lv. Syracuse		12.10 P.M.	5.30 P.M.	6.50 P.M.
" Warner		12.45 "	.....	7.17 "
" Memphis		1.00 "	.....	7.27 "
" Jordan		1.29 "	.....	7.47 "
" Weedsport		1.57 "	.....	8.05 "
Ar. Port Byron		2.02 "	.....	8.10 "
Lv. Port Byron		4.00 P.M.	.....	8.00 A.M.
Ar. Auburn		4.25 "	.....	8.25 "
Lv. Auburn		9.15 A.M.	.....	5.35 P.M.
Ar. Port Byron		9.37 "	.....	6.00 "
Lv. Port Byron	7.07 A.M.	2.27 P.M.	.....	8.20 "
" Montezuma	7.16 "	2.35 "	.....	.....
" Savannah	7.28 "	2.57 "	.....	8.43 "
" Clyde	7.45 "	3.27 "	.....	9.12 "
" Locke Berlin	7.51 "	3.33 "	.....	.....
" Lyons	8.02 "	4.13 "	.....	9.48 "
Ar. Newark	8.15 "	4.29 "	.....	10.03 "
Lv. Newark	8.20 "	5.15 "	.....	10.23 "
" Port Gibson	8.32 "	5.30 "	.....	10.32 "
" Palmyra	9.08 "	6.05 "	.....	10.55 "
" Macedon	9.17 "	6.20 "	.....	.....
" Egypt	9.25 "	6.28 "	.....	.....
" Fairport	9.40 "	7.30 "	.....	11.40 "
" E. Rochester	9.50 "	.....	.....	.....
" E. Blvd. Road	10.00 "	8.00 "	.....	12.00 "
Ar. Rochester	10.15 "	8.15 "	8.15 "	12.20 "

(Columns 305: WELLS FARGO & CO. EXPRESS and ROCHESTER THROUGH FREIGHT)

Train 300 daily except Sunday and Holidays.
Train 302-306 daily except Sunday. On Holidays Newark to Syracuse only.
Train 304-308 daily except Sunday and holidays.
Train 310 daily except Sunday and holidays.
Train 301 daily. Runs to East Boulevard road only on Sunday.
Train 303 daily except Sunday. On holidays Syracuse to Newark only.
Train 305-307 daily except Sunday and holidays.
* Train 300 will stop at stations not scheduled above upon request at the General Freight Agent's office.

NORTHBOUND	1-3	41-45-49-53-55
Lv. Syracuse	* 4.20 A.M.	* 12.40 P.M.
" Long Branch	.....	1.05 "
" Baldwinsville	.....	1.55 "
" Phoenix	.....	2.30 "
" Fulton	5.55 "	3.16 "
" Minettto	.....	3.40 "
Ar. Oswego	6.25 "	3.55 "

* Will stop at stations not scheduled to deliver perishable shipments only. Carries trailer, Syracuse to Fulton.

SOUTHBOUND	24-26-30-34-38	76-80
Lv. Oswego	8.23 A.M.	* 6.03 P.M.
" Minetto	8.50 "	6.18 "
" Fulton	9.29 "	6.54 "
" Phoenix	10.14 "	7.18 "
" Baldwinsville	10.50 "	7.32 "
" Long Branch	11.04 "	7.44 "
Ar. Syracuse	11.28 "	8.07 "

* Carries trailer, Fulton to Syracuse.

Close connections are made with the Syracuse and South Bay Electric R. R. Co., and Syracuse, Watertown and St. Lawrence River R. R. Co., at Syracuse, for North Syracuse, Cicero, Brewerton and South Bay.

Auburn & Syracuse Electric R. R. at Auburn for Skaneateles, Marcellus and Split Rock.

New York State Railways (Oneida Lines) at Syracuse for Utica, Rome, Little Falls and all intermediate points.

Buffalo, Lockport and Rochester Railways at Rochester for all points between Rochester and Lockport.

INSTRUCTIONS TO SHIPPERS.

Freight houses are open for the receipt and delivery of freight daily except Sundays and holidays as follows:

Auburn ....7.00 A.M. to 6.00 P.M.
Rochester ....7.00 A.M. to 5.00 P.M.
Syracuse ....7.00 A.M. to 5.30 P.M.
All other stations....7.00 A.M. to 6.00 P.M.

On the foregoing time tables are shown the leaving times of all freight cars. Freight shipments must be delivered to freight houses between the hours mentioned above and at **terminal stations at least 30 minutes** and at all other points **15 minutes** before the leaving time as shown on schedule.

The Company reserves the right to change schedule without notice to the public, and does not guarantee to forward shipments upon any particular train.

An experienced man will call upon you at your request and explain our service and just how it is best adapted to your needs.

For rates, maps and further information apply to

LOCAL AGENTS, or

H. C. Stanton, General Freight Agent

S. W. Bullock, Commercial Freight Agent

Syracuse, N. Y. (Telephone Warren 4980)

↑This poster, greatly reduced from the original, told shippers how and when to use the service. They already knew why if they had already tried the "slower steam routes." The nightly trains in the schedule were often two or three cars including trailers from connecting lines. J. R. MCFARLANE

After the A&S gave in to the hard-surfaced roads on April 15, 1930, through freight and express were routed over the Rochester & Syracuse and Auburn & Northern via Port Byron until those lines were discontinued a year later.

Rochester Area

One of the most extensive electric railway properties in the state was the *New York State Railways* with nearly 340 route miles and over 580 miles of track. Two of its interurban divisions radiated from Rochester: the *Rochester & Sodus Bay Line* extending 41 miles easterly to Sodus Point on Lake Ontario and the *Rochester & Eastern Line* (R&E) extending 44 miles southeasterly to Canandaigua (kan-en-DAY-gwa) and Geneva in the heart of the Finger Lakes region.

The Sodus line, a single-track side-of-the-road trolley through a prosperous fruit growing area, opened August 22, 1900. Inbound express consisted of eggs, dressed meat, fresh fruit, milk and other provisions. Outbound shipments were bread, ice cream, produce and merchandise consigned to small stores in the numerous towns and villages along the line. No carload traffic was handled because the line closely paralleled the "R. W. & O. Division" of the New York Central.

The R&E line to Geneva was also a single-track operation but was located mostly on private right-of-way. Local express traffic was heaviest outbound from Rochester, principally merchandise for outlying merchants. The R&E maintained track connections with the New York Central at Pittsford, the Lehigh Valley at Victor and the Northern Central (Pennsylvania) Railroad near Seneca Castle. The interurban received a flat rate for each steam road car handled. Because of lack of on-line industries, revenue from this source was small. Scattered carloads of coal, bagged cement, etc., were the principal commodities handled.

Prior to World War I, both the Sodus and R&E lines offered two classes of local express service. Class "A" provided transportation plus wagon pick-up and delivery service in Rochester and the larger on-line towns. "A" rates were equivalent to those of old-line express companies and the goods were carried on regular passenger cars. Independent cartage agents were employed, those in the outlying towns being paid on a commission basis—20% of the class "A" revenue. The agent in Rochester was paid a flat rate for the service. In addition, the interurbans furnished him two "elec-

↑**From 1904 to 1909, the line to Geneva was called the *Rochester & Eastern Rapid Railway*. Really it ran *south*east from Rochester. Car #925, a box motor with an open rear platform, is on Monroe at Highland Avenue in Rochester.** WILLIAM REED GORDON COLLECTION VIA J. R. MCFARLANE

tric automobile delivery wagons" for exclusive use of railway shipments. Class "B" was rail transportation only. The "B" rates were 3¢ to 5¢ per 100 pounds higher than steam road charges. This class of express moved in standard freight motors.

The R&E and Sodus lines used a common freight terminal in downtown Rochester but until 1921, it was separate from the one used by the interurbans from Syracuse and Lockport.

The Sodus line was an early victim of the paved roads. Last cars were operated to Sodus Point on June 27, 1929. The R&E continued little more than a year before folding on July 31, 1930.

The *Rochester Subway* (officially the *Rapid Transit and Industrial Railway*) was owned by the city of Rochester and operated under a service-at-cost contract by the *Rochester Lines* of *New York State Railways*. The 9-mile subway was built in the abandoned bed of the original Erie Canal as it passed through Rochester in a northwesterly-southeasterly direction. Opened December 1, 1927, the line was designed to remove the Lockport, Syracuse and Geneva interurban passenger cars from the streets and to provide a local passenger and freight service as well. The interurbans' passenger cars used the subway, but their freight motors continued to travel the streets in order to reach the union freight terminal on North Plymouth Avenue near downtown Rochester.

About eight city blocks of the subway through downtown Rochester was roofed over and named

Broad Street. The balance was in open cut. Two tracks were for passenger service and a third for freight. Track connections were made with New York Central (at two locations), Lehigh Valley and Baltimore & Ohio (B&O) railroads. Through the Lehigh Valley, cars could also be interchanged with the Erie and Pennsylvania railroads.

Forty to fifty industries were located along the old canal bed, but only about two dozen took advantage of the subway and had sidings installed or shared one with others. One of the principal subway customers was the Rochester *Times Union* newspaper. The New York State Barge Canal Terminal could be reached by the subway over a short electrified section of the Lehigh Valley.

The subway had one electric locomotive, a 50-ton steeple-cab (#L-1) built in the New York State Railways Rochester shops with parts purchased from General Electric. Backup power was #0205, an express motor from the Rochester & Eastern Line. In the first ten years of operation, about 44,000 cars were handled in the subway. Freight revenues in 1929 were about $37,000.

New York State Railways—Rochester Lines transferred its property to *Rochester Transit Corporation* on August 2, 1938. By the 1950's the populace considered the subway antique and they were clamoring for a superhighway along the route. Passenger operation in the subway ceased June 30, 1956 but electric switching continued until September 2, 1957. The eastern half of the subway was converted into Interstate highway 490.

↓**Passing #L-1 is Rochester Transit #48, once a Rome–Little Falls interurban. It approaches General Motors loop, the west end of the subway.** THOMAS J. DWORMAN

↑**Rochester Transit #L-1 pushes a train on May 12, 1956. Characteristics of the subway which show up in this view include heavy catenary construction, General Railway Signal Company block signals for left-hand running, and usually a luxuriant growth of weeds.** STEPHEN D. MAGUIRE COLLECTION

At the west end, the B&O built a connection into the General Motors complex and the city replaced several cross-street bridges with solid fill. About half a mile of subway track remained underground in the mid-1980's for use by the Chessie (ex-B&O), connecting its local freight yard near West Main Street with the *Times Union* siding opposite old City Hall station of the subway.

The *Erie Railroad* electrified 34 miles of its Rochester Division passenger service from Rochester south to Mount Morris on June 18, 1907. Carload freight was handled by steam locomotives. This was the time in history when steam railroads were experimenting with various types and voltages of electrification as it was fully expected that the electric age was arriving. Erie was the first railroad in the country to electrify with single-phase 25-cycle current at 11,000 volts. Three of the eight passenger motor cars were combines and thus accommodated a modest LCL package and express business. Electric service ended November 29, 1934.

The *Rochester & Manitou Railroad* (opened May 30, 1891 as *Grand View Beach Railroad* and named *Rochester, Charlotte & Manitou Railroad*, 1895–1908) was a 7½-mile single-track summer-only operation along Lake Ontario. The eastern terminus was at Ontario Beach (Charlotte), the north end of New York State Railways' Lake Avenue Line from Rochester. Manitou Beach on the

↑**Rochester & Manitou car #25, used to haul freight and work trailers, had two 60-horse GE-87 motors and no air brakes. Imagine trying to control trailers with only hand brakes!** RICHARD R. ANDREWS COLLECTION

west end was a summer resort reached by laying the track along the beach strips and crossing several inlets on pile trestles, one 3,000 feet in length.

Baggage and express for the cottage dwellers along the way were handled by a locally built single-truck work car (#25) and several single-truck trailers. The company had one industrial siding, into the Rochester waterworks, located a mile or so west of Ontario Beach. Another early victim of the automobile, all service on the electric road ended in the late fall of 1924.

The *Buffalo, Lockport & Rochester Railway* (BL&R) was a first-class high-speed single-track interurban between Lockport and Rochester. After April 1919 it was the *Rochester, Lockport & Buffalo Railroad* (RL&B).

The 54½-mile line was opened November 17, 1908. Cars entered Lockport over International Railway Company track and Rochester over the Lyell Avenue line of New York State Railways beginning in May 1910. The interurban route was sandwiched between the Erie Barge Canal and the Falls Road of the New York Central, all passing through a very prosperous fruit and vegetable producing district. Sidings were constructed by the interurban to serve the State School at Albion and four canneries at various points on the line.

Local freight and express were handled by two Niles-built express motors. A third unit was added in 1916. The roster included five home-built freight box trailers. The company also had 11 flat cars equipped with side boards for carrying produce to the canneries. Carload freight interchanged from steam roads was limited to coal received from the Buffalo, Rochester & Pittsburgh Railway (B&O) at the Rochester car barn interchange track for delivery to the State School power plant at Albion.

In January 1914, crews of the BL&R began operating their own cars all the way through to Buffalo over International Railway Company tracks from Lockport. The freight cars terminated

↓**It's August 1919 and the Rochester, Lockport & Buffalo has taken over from an earlier company, but express motor #301 hasn't been relettered. It is at the Erie Railroad freight house on Exchange Street, Rochester. In 1921, the RL&B will move to a new union freight terminal of the New York State Railways.** W. A. LUCAS VIA J. R. MCFARLANE

↑**International Railway #3 later became #81 of the Toledo & Eastern Railroad.** J. R. MC FARLANE COLLECTION

↓**Stranger than fiction! The text on page 114 tells why the caboose has a trolley.** J. R. MC FARLANE COLLECTION

at the Buffalo & Lake Erie Traction Company freight house on Swan Street, south of the business district. The Rochester terminal at the Erie Railroad freight house was shared with the Rochester & Syracuse line. Later that year, Wells Fargo express service was instituted between Rochester and Buffalo.

The RL&B was an early victim of the Great Depression when people stopped riding the cars. The company's freight and express business was insufficient to hold the road together and all operations ceased April 30, 1931.

Niagara Frontier

The *International Railway Company* (IRC) operated a major streetcar and interurban system. It boasted more than 100 miles of street railway routes in Buffalo, Niagara Falls and Lockport, 45 miles of interurban lines connecting those points plus a dozen route miles in the Falls section of Canada. In the year 1912, the IRC reported hauling 243,500 tons of freight and express, more than twice the amount hauled by any other trolley freight operation in the state.

In 1899, the *Buffalo & Lockport Railway,* a predecessor to the IRC, leased a 13-mile-long branch of the Erie Railroad between Lockport and North Tonawanda (11 miles north of downtown Buffalo). The Erie Railroad line and associated industrial sidings in Lockport were then electrified and a further 16-mile extension was constructed north from Lockport to reach Olcott Beach on Lake Ontario.

Two 1899-vintage steeple-cab locomotives (#1–2) spearheaded a standard railroad freight operation between North Tonawanda and Olcott. Most of the industries in Lockport were served by the IRC. Interchange with the Erie was made at North Tonawanda with billing through the Erie switching tariff. In the early years there was also an interchange with the New York Central at Lockport. Much on-line freight was generated in the Lockport-Olcott fruit belt prior to the mid-1920's. Fruit motors and trailers by the trainload ran to the Lockport canneries and to the wholesale markets in Buffalo.

In 1913, the locomotive roster was supplemented by a standard Baldwin-Westinghouse 50-ton job (#3). The company also possessed ten 40- to 50-foot double-truck freight motors and a dozen 34- to 38-foot double-truck box trailers. Last, but not least, was the #N-7, a single-truck caboose with one powered axle and a trolley pole! It was indeed a singular sight to see a freight train being made up in the Lockport yard and watch the caboose move down the track under its own power and couple itself to the rear of the train.

Passenger service on the Buffalo-Lockport-Olcott Division was discontinued on October 30, 1937. The electric locomotives continued the carload freight business until January 31, 1951 when the Erie's bankruptcy caused cancellation of the 99-year lease with the IRC and the road was dieselized. The line between North Tonawanda and Lockport continued through the years to become Conrail's Lockport Branch.

Trolley freight operation over the balance of the IRC was pretty much limited to carloads of fruit moving in the first decade of the 1900's from the Lewiston-Youngstown area on the lower Niagara River to the Buffalo markets. The route was over the Niagara Gorge Railroad and the IRC's Buffalo–Niagara Falls Division. Baggage cars were scheduled over both the Lockport and Niagara Falls interurban divisions up to the time of World War I.

↓**Leaving Olcott (N. Y.) circa 1913, International Railway #Q-2 with eight fruit trailers pauses at Olcott Junction, where a short branch from the Olcott Beach amusement park joined the line from town.** MORRIS H. LLOYD COLLECTION

↑Locomotive #1 of the Buffalo & Lockport Railway was built in 1899 by General Electric Company. The International Railway still conducted an electric operation until 1951 with this same locomotive. That was no record life for a steeple-cab, but it was a long time for a locomotive to serve on a single railway! DUKE-MIDDLETON COLLECTION

The *Niagara Gorge Railroad* was originally opened in July 1895 as the *Niagara Falls & Lewiston Railroad.* It went under the hammer in 1899 and emerged with its later name. The double-track scenic route along both the American and Canadian sides of the Niagara River became really effective as a tourist attraction that same summer when the Canadian line, the *Niagara Falls Park & River Railway* (opened in 1893) came under the same management. Freight service on the Niagara Gorge was not so significant as it was really an extension of the Lewiston & Youngstown Frontier Railway.

↓Niagara Gorge #61 handled baggage on trains that met Toronto steamers. RICHARD R. ANDREWS COLLECTION

The *Lewiston & Youngstown Frontier Railway* (L&Y) was a 7.3-mile electric line connecting Fort Niagara and Youngstown at the mouth of the Niagara River with Lewiston on the New York Central and Niagara Gorge railroads. Carload freight was hauled from the opening day, August 8, 1896.

Motive power consisted of a 6-ton-capacity single-truck Brill box motor 14 feet long. This unit was fitted with standard railroad-type couplers as well as radial drawbars for pulling streetcars. Principal commodities transported were fruit outbound in steam road reefers and coal inbound for Fort Niagara. In the early 1900's, the L&Y originated many fruit express electric trains for movement over the Niagara Gorge Railroad and International Railway Company to Buffalo. A 1911 *Official Guide* indicated a baggage car operation between Niagara Falls and Youngstown for connection with boats on Lake Ontario for St. Lawrence River points.

Passenger service on the L&Y was given up in 1924 but electric freight continued until 1937 using a 40-foot box motor leased from the neighboring Niagara Gorge Railroad. The road was operated with diesel power until complete abandonment in 1950.

↑Niagara Junction Railway #4 and #3, seen on July 14, 1914, were the road's first two electrics in 1913, Baldwin-Westinghouse Class D locomotives. They must have been satisfactory, for NJ ordered three similar units in 1916–1937. In 1920 NJ got two smaller Class B's which were sold off after "only" 26 years. GEORGE KRAMBLES COLLECTION

The *Niagara Junction Railway* (NJ) operation could hardly have been considered trolley freight for it was a first-class heavy-duty electric railroad owning 11 miles of main line and 33 miles of yard tracks located entirely within the city of Niagara Falls. The nearly two dozen industries on the line owned an additional 19 miles of side tracks. No passenger service was ever operated—that certainly distinguished it from most electric lines!

The NJ was built in 1892 to deliver materials for construction of Niagara Falls Power Company's hydro-electric generating plant. The railroad was routed through power company land which was gradually sold to industries requiring large amounts of inexpensive electricity. The NJ, of course, served the industries. Originally operated with steam locomotives, the NJ was electrified in 1913. It then operated about 5 miles of main line and 8 miles of sidings. Two 50-ton electric locomotives and two flat cars handled all the work.

As the industrial district expanded and the railroad grew, additional motive power was acquired. Until the end of electrified service, six or seven GE center-cab locomotives built in 1952 were kept busy 24 hours a day moving approximately 3,500 freight cars per month.

The locomotives drew 600-volt DC power through pantographs from single catenary overhead. Most sidings were electrified but where overhead wire was lacking for safety reasons the NJ used reacher cars to set empties and lift loads.

The only piece of motorized rolling stock on the railroad other than the locomotives was #1, a line car built by Brill as a passenger car seventy years before and still running on its original trucks.

In 1948, the power company sold the NJ to three railroads with which it interchanged, 50% to the New York Central and 25% each to the Lehigh Valley and Erie. Having consolidated all of these, Conrail is the present (1992) owner. Diesels were substituted for the electric operation in mid-November 1980. Even at that late date, electric locomotives had continued value. Two were transferred to Conrail to work around Grand Central Terminal in New York City. Another serves today (1992) to haul work trains for the Port Authority Transit Corporation in the Philadelphia area.

↓The headlight in the rear belongs to a pusher which will assist this 17-car transfer drag from Gill Creek Yard, along the Niagara River, up the 1.5% grade to the railroad interchange at Foote Yard. All of these points are within Niagara Falls (N. Y.) KEN KRAEMER

↑Niagara Junction Railway locomotives #17 and #18 (in the distance) shift cars in Foote Yard. These are two of the 1952-built General Electric steeple-cabs which eventually closed out the electric era on Niagara Junction. FRED W. SCHNEIDER III

One of the major links in the trolley freight chain across central and western New York state was the 93-mile *Buffalo & Lake Erie Traction Company* (B&LET). This single-track line was built along the south shore of Lake Erie to connect Buffalo with Erie (Pa.). East of Dunkirk, the track was located on private right-of-way. West of Fredonia, it was a relatively high-speed roadside line.

Starting with three standard express motors, the company added three more by 1912. Local express business through the "Grape Belt" increased steadily so that in the years 1910–1919, the B&LET purchased 15 express trailers. Local freight was hauled at rates 10%–25% higher than steam road rates. By 1925 this spread had been reduced to parity. The company operated a pick-up and delivery service in Buffalo, Dunkirk, Fredonia and Erie. Rates were 5¢ per 100 pounds with a 35¢ minimum for either pick-up or delivery. Joint tariffs were in effect between all points on the B&LET and Chautauqua Traction Company. Similar tariffs were written with the Jamestown, Westfield & Northwestern Railroad when that line was electrified and placed in service in 1914. Jamestown was a center for furniture making and considerable amounts of those products were handled in electric motors and trailers to points on the B&LET. The traction was not equipped to haul steam road cars at any point on its line.

The B&LET management was not one to turn down a revenue dollar. During the early 1920's when automobiles were becoming more numerous but parts of the main highways were still hub-deep in mud during early spring, the traction company posted signs on the main road near the New York–Pennsylvania border reading ROAD IMPASSABLE. WE WILL MOVE YOUR AUTO TO GOOD ROAD FOR $5.00. The trip was 6 miles and a freight motor and flat car ran every hour, taking four autos at a time.

American Express Company operated on the B&LET prior to World War I, but only between Dunkirk and Fredonia. This unusual situation probably occurred because Fredonia was the only reasonably large intermediate population center not located on the main line of either New York Central or Nickel Plate. In 1916 Wells Fargo contracted to operate over the entire interurban line.

↓The Erie (Pa.) Automobile Club asked Buffalo & Lake Erie Traction to provide automobile ferry service along Lake Shore highway through Ripley (N.Y.). There was a seasonal need! Up to 31 autos were carried in a single day. WILLIAM REED GORDON COLLECTION

←**Buffalo & Lake Erie Traction #C-2 at Fredonia (N.Y.) circa 1910. B&LET made this unit from a box car of the Jamestown, Chautauqua & Lake Erie Railway, a steam shortline which only later would itself be electrified.** LEONARD Y. TRIPP

←**Buffalo & Lake Erie #C-4 (like #C-3) was built new by the Cincinnati Car Company in 1910. Here it is in front of Fredonia barn. Non-passenger cars were often designated by "letter and number" on Mitten Management properties. B&LET may have been influenced by the nearby International Railway, a Mitten line.** LEONARD Y. TRIPP, FRED W. SCHNEIDER III COLLECTION

On January 1, 1925, the *Buffalo & Erie Railway* (B&E) took over the faltering B&LET. The new company was destined to have only one or two good revenue years. The bottom fell out of the local freight business due to a mid-1925 decision of the U. S. Supreme Court which negated rulings of the Pennsylvania and New York public utility commissions prohibiting local truck competition with the interurbans. As hordes of independent truckers hit the roads, the B&E local freight revenues dropped from 21% of total income in 1924 to 12% in 1927, even though interline freight percentages increased from 5% in 1924 to 11% in 1927. Because of the change in mix of the freight business, the B&E was able to sell two express motors (#C-3 and #C-4) to the Southern New York Railway, where they became #215 and #214. The B&E went into receivership in 1928 and ceased main line operation on January 27, 1933.

Jamestown and the Chautauqua Lake Area

Jamestown, at the foot of Chautauqua Lake in the southwestern corner of New York state, was served only by the Erie Railroad, so much of the electric railway construction in the region was made to overcome the disadvantage of being a one-railroad town. The *Jamestown Street Railway* operated a baggage and express service in connection with American Express Company on the 3-mile suburban line to Falconer in order to connect with the Dunkirk, Allegheny Valley & Pittsburgh Railroad (New York Central).

The owners of the Jamestown Street Railway also built the 29-mile *Chautauqua Traction Company* (CT) along the west shore of Chautauqua Lake from Lakewood to Westfield for connections with the main lines of the New York Central and

Nickel Plate railroads. By 1912, the CT was earning a healthy 11% of its revenues from hauling mail, express and baggage. American Express Company also operated on the CT. Cars were not interchanged with the steam roads but the company did have joint tariffs of class and commodity rates for less-than-carload lots with the Buffalo & Lake Erie Traction Company. CT with its predominantly passenger traffic was eclipsed by the Jamestown, Westfield & Northwestern Railroad and so faded from the scene on March 20, 1926.

Competition for the CT was the Jamestown, Chautauqua & Lake Erie Railway, a steam road along the east side of Chautauqua Lake. In 1913, the Jamestown Street Railway interests purchased and electrified the steam line under the name of *Jamestown, Westfield & Northwestern Railroad* (JW&NW). This 32-mile line survived all other interurbans in New York state by reason of its heavy carload freight and express business.

New York–Jamestown mail via the New York Central was carried by the electric line, it being a service superior to the shorter Jamestown–Jersey City (N. J.) route via the Erie.

First American Express and finally the Railway Express Agency operated over the JW&NW. Through freight service and daily merchandise cars to all important commercial centers were offered in connection with the New York Central and Nickel Plate at Westfield and the Pennsylvania Railroad at Mayville. Through rates were published with all trunk lines.

JW&NW service began September 12, 1914 with baggage cars #306 and #307 built by Cincinnati and a Baldwin-Westinghouse 45-ton steeple-cab locomotive (#400). In 1927 a similar home-built locomotive (#500) appeared on the scene followed three years later by #300, an express motor from the Detroit United Railway. The ex–Southern New York Railway #80 (ex–Albany Southern #27) was rebuilt by JW&NW as #320, a line car and plow. A four-wheel caboose (#409) rounded out the freight fleet. The heaviest grade on the JW&NW, replete with several **S** curves, was about 7 miles long from Main Street, Westfield, up to Parkers. Chautauqua Lake lies about 800 feet above the level of Lake Erie. Maximum load for #400 or #500 was 275 tons when operating separately or 400 tons when doubleheading.

World War II served to stay the demise of the electrified JW&NW until November 30, 1947 when the diesels took over. That operation lasted only until January 21, 1950, then the line was dismantled.

The neighboring *Warren & Jamestown Street Railway* operated half of its 20-mile line in New York state. Despite its small size, it earned a place among the state's top ten in trolley freight (LCL) revenues earned in 1912. It had no track connection with the Jamestown Street Railway. In 1911 it was offering double-daily baggage and express trips between its terminals. Wells Fargo operated over the road. This little line expired on December 2, 1929.

→Jamestown, Westfield & Northwestern Railroad express car #300 hauls freight cars south at Bay View (N. Y.), April 29, 1939. JAMES P. SHUMAN

Interline Trolley Freight

By far the most successful interline trolley freight route in New York state connected Syracuse with Buffalo, 169 miles. In 1911, the Buffalo, Lockport & Rochester (BL&R) came under control of the Beebe Syndicate, which in turn controlled the Rochester, Syracuse & Eastern (RS&E), the Syracuse, Lake Shore & Northern, the Auburn & Syracuse, the Syracuse & South Bay and the Auburn & Northern. With the collapse of the Beebe Syndicate in 1917, the roads went their separate ways but those operating out of Syracuse continued to share much common management.

In 1914, the BL&R obtained running rights for its freight cars over the 25 miles of International Railway Company tracks between Lockport (otherwise its westernmost terminus) and Buffalo. Thereafter, for tariff purposes, Buffalo was considered a station on the BL&R. The Buffalo terminal was that of the Buffalo & Lake Erie Traction Company (B&LET) on Swan Street where all loads were transferred until the tenants began through freight operations in 1924.

In May of 1915, the Empire United Railways (reorganized RS&E) inaugurated a fast package freight service via Rochester to over fifty points in western New York served by steam trains of the Erie Railroad. Merchandise was transferred at the steam road's freight house, which was also the Rochester terminal for Empire United and BL&R.

The move to develop interline LCL traffic via trolley freight finally got under way following World War I. The 1918 consolidation of the four main line express companies into American Railway Express undoubtedly did much to foster closer relationships between the freight departments of the electric lines.

On November 3, 1919, through electric freight runs were inaugurated between Syracuse and Buffalo. Shipments of freight received at each terminal before 4:30 or 5:00 in the afternoon were available for next morning delivery at the other terminal. In later years it was not uncommon to see four- or five-car freight trains leaving the Syracuse, Rochester or Buffalo terminals. Westbound loadings were heavier than eastbound and the more distant hauls were less susceptible to truck competition prior to completion of the state's paved road system.

Ward Baking Company of Syracuse was a steady customer of the electrics. Auto parts were shipped from Brown Lipe Chapin in Syracuse to the Pierce Arrow Company in Buffalo. A nice business in perishable fruits from the Oswego River valley was built up as the company advertised first morning delivery in Buffalo. Window shades made near Oswego moved with regularity to points on the Rochester & Syracuse. Pianos manufactured in East Rochester were frequently sent by interurban to the Buffalo area. BL&R trailers were loaded with electrical parts at the Locke Insulator Company in Victor on the Rochester & Eastern Line of New York State Railways and were hauled to Niagara Falls. Some freight traffic was developed between the heavy manufacturing plants in Buffalo and Auburn. For a time, trailer loads of compressors originating in Utica were hauled over the New York State Railways—Oneida Line to Syracuse, thence to Buffalo via the three connecting interurbans. Less than 24 hours was required for the trip.

There was no regular interchange of trolley freight between the lines east and west of Syracuse and no through rates were ever published. Express cars from Utica and from Rochester did not even share a common terminal in Syracuse.

In 1921, a new electric railway union freight terminal was opened in Rochester. Eleven cars could be docked. Tenants were the Rochester, Lockport & Buffalo (ex-BL&R), Rochester & Syracuse Railroad (R&S) plus the Rochester & Eastern and Rochester & Sodus Bay lines of New York State Railways. By January of 1923, these tenants, together with the Empire State Railroad (a reorganization of the Syracuse, Lake Shore & Northern and the Empire United) and Auburn & Syracuse, joined in issuing freight tariffs of class and commodity rates. In March of the following year, the B&LET joined the group. Resulting tariffs indicated through rates between Oswego and Syracuse in the east and points as far west as the B&LET, the Jamestown, Westfield & Northwestern and the Northwestern Pennsylvania Electric Service Company (the line south from Erie).

One of the first freight traffic efforts made by the new Buffalo & Erie Railway after its January 1925 reorganization of B&LET was to establish through rates with the Cleveland, Painesville & Eastern Railroad, the Lake Shore Electric Railway, the Cleveland Southwestern Railway & Light Company and the Northern Ohio Traction & Light Company. Trucks of the Buffalo & Erie Coach Corporation (a railway subsidiary) operated between Erie (Pa.) and Ashtabula (Ohio) because the interurban links between those two points had been broken in 1922. This new service was expensive to operate and was quickly doomed by the abandonment of the Cleveland-Painesville-Ashtabula line in the spring of 1926.

The R&S worked out a somewhat more practical albeit seasonal arrangement to reach distant points via three boat lines. Through rates were published with the Rutland–Lake Michigan Transit Company between points on the R&S and Chicago or Milwaukee via the Empire State Railroad and Oswego on Lake Ontario. Little is known of this circuitous operation which lasted only two seasons. The boats did not operate in 1926 and the rates were cancelled. There were also joint rates, via RL&B and Buffalo, with the Detroit & Cleveland Navigation Company to reach Detroit and with the Cleveland & Buffalo Transit Company to reach Cleveland. Joint rates with these two lines were cancelled at the close of navigation in 1929.

The main stem of trolley freight across western New York was broken when the Rochester, Lockport & Buffalo ceased April 30, 1931. Two months later, the Empire State and R&S quit. The interurbans became a thing of the past.

↑ **Hudson Valley Railway car #254, seen in Glens Falls, was built in 1901 for the new express service of the Electric Express Company.** J. R. MCFARLANE COLLECTION

Express Companies on the Interurbans

In addition to their own express business, a number of the interurbans in New York state signed contracts with one or another of the four old-line express companies, thus extending the electric roads' potential express market far beyond their own lines. The express business of the old-line companies was consolidated into American Railway Express in 1918. This action was fatal to interurban participation as the new company was steam railroad–oriented. One exception was to be found in the Jamestown, Westfield & Northwestern Railroad which had a contract with the Railway Express Agency as long as the electric cars operated.

The only interline express company "captive" to the interurbans in New York state was the *Electric Express Company*. Organized in 1901, this concern operated a joint service over Schenectady Railway, United Traction Company (in the Albany and Troy area) and the Hudson Valley Railway. Each railway rented express cars and freight stations to Electric Express for fixed sums per year and furnished crews and power for 20¢–25¢ per car mile, loaded or empty. Until 1909, free drayage was provided. Two scheduled freight cars were operated daily on the Albany-Troy and Albany-Schenectady lines of Schenectady Railway and over the Troy–Glens Falls and Troy-Stillwater lines of the Hudson Valley Railway. This pooling arrangement was discontinued in 1918 as it was felt the individual lines could run their own operations better.

Perhaps they could . . . or is it symbolic that this look at trolley freight ends on that note?

Not Only Passengers is intended to show *how* the electric railways carried the goods. It might also be asked—*where* and *how much* did they carry?

Electric railways had been built mostly in populous regions, so their freight was concentrated there. About 85% of the nation's electric railway revenue for freight, mail and express was earned in only 18 of the then 48 states, as shown in the circle graph for 1917–1927. California is especially noteworthy as in 1920 it had only 3.2% of the population. You can see that New England's share peaked early. The central states—especially Ohio—and scattered states elsewhere did well in the 1920's. During 1927–1937, after the period shown in the graph, decline in both the electric railway industry and the national economy brought freight revenue down by 47%. Even so, Colorado, Iowa, Oklahoma and Texas were real success stories as they each had more revenue in actual dollars in 1937 than in 1927.

Distribution of freight, express and mail revenue by region (100% = entire United States)

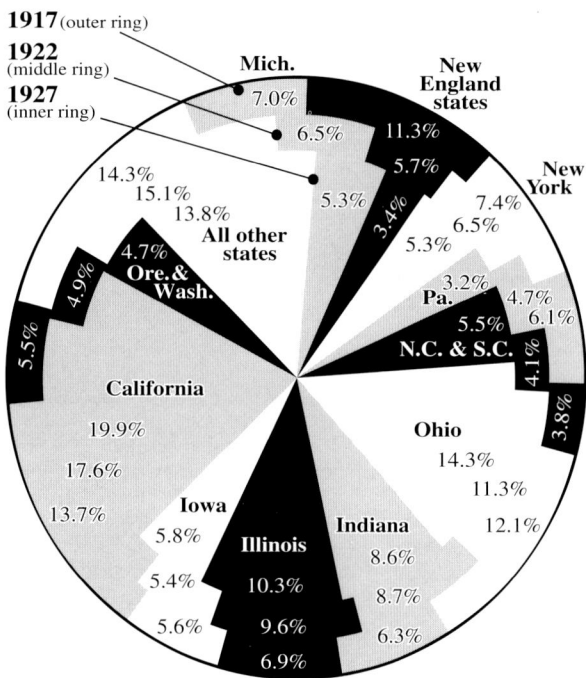

1917 (outer ring)
1922 (middle ring)
1927 (inner ring)

Mich.
7.0%
6.5%
5.3%

New England states
11.3%
5.7%

New York
7.4%
6.5%
5.3%

14.3%
15.1%
13.8%

All other states

4.7%
Ore. & Wash.
4.9%
5.5%

3.4%

3.2%
4.7%
6.1%
Pa.
5.5%
N.C. & S.C.
4.1%
3.8%

California
19.9%
17.6%
13.7%

Ohio
14.3%
11.3%
12.1%

Iowa
5.8%
5.4%
5.6%

Illinois
10.3%
9.6%
6.9%

Indiana
8.6%
8.7%
6.3%

And how much revenue was there? About $40 million annually (back when a million dollars was a million dollars). Adjusted for inflation, this would amount to about $300 million in 1992 dollars.

About This Book

The impetus for Central Electric Railfans' Association to produce nationwide coverage of "trolley freight" came years ago, in 1974. It was Jack Keenan's wonderfully sensitive description of one railway's freight activity in *Cincinnati & Lake Erie Railroad, Ohio's Great Interurban System.* A great deal of material was quickly collected, thanks to members and friends of CERA with a particular interest in one line or another. So much information and so many illustrations came forth, in fact, that it was not evident how a book of reasonable size could encompass the

subject. A workable solution that would meet the goal of offering general—not just local or regional—coverage proved elusive. Along the way, however, the project gained a title expressing the fact that the electric railways' traffic was "not only passengers."

Eventually, in 1991, CERA bit the bullet and recognized that the solution was to treat local methods of handling freight as examples of nationwide practices rather than as isolated developments to be extensively described in their own right. This conclusion permitted Roy Benedict to build on the work of the previous editorial managers—Norm Carlson and Fred Schneider—and others. The final result was to bring *Not Only Passengers* to realization.

CERA founding member George Krambles was instrumental in this book. He rounded up a great deal of reference material during the early years of the project and also provided much of the background knowledge of both the transit and publishing industries which underlies the final product. Others who provided data include Joseph M. Canfield, Norman Carlson, Terence W. Cassidy, Raymond DeGroote, Robert E. Geis, Richard R. Hofer, Richard R. Kunz, F. C. (Lyle) LeGrove, Leon B. Levine, James S. Levis, Robert J. Levis, Richard Lukin, John E. Merriken, Arthur H. Peterson, John P. Scharle, Anthony J. Schill, Fred W. Schneider, III, William M. Shapotkin, James P. Shuman and John R. Wilmot. Contributors of some specific items are recognized in "Notes and Sources," pages 123–124. Photos are credited where they appear, if possible to the original photographer and the collector who loaned CERA a print. This book has been so long in preparation that regrettably several of the contributors must be recognized posthumously.

Not Only Passengers was designed and electronically prepared for publication by Roy G. Benedict Publishers' Services, Chicago, Illinois. Halftones and printing negatives were by Jim Walter Color Separations, Beloit, Wisconsin; printing and binding by Walsworth Publishing, Marceline, Missouri.

During 1991–1992 while this book was in production, the CERA directors were: Phillip F. Cioffi, Walter R. Keevil, Frederick D. Lonnes, Donald L. MacCorquodale, Bruce Moffat, Stanford A. Nettis, William Reynolds, David Sadowski, William M. Shapotkin, Jeffrey L. Wien and David Wilson.

y's Work

↑**The day's freight run just completed is shrouded in the haze of fatigue from a job well done as the crew leaves their motor, Fort Wayne–Lima Railroad #33. The location is Fort Wayne (Ind.) in 1928 or 1929.**
GEORGE K. BRADLEY COLLECTION

CERA bulletins are technical, educational historical studies by members of the Central Electric Railfans' Association, working without salary, with particular knowledge and interest in the subject. CERA is an Illinois not-for-profit corporation. This book is consistent with CERA's purpose of fostering the study of the history, equipment and operation of electric railways. Any reader having information correcting that contained in *Not Only Passengers* is invited to send documentation in support thereof, citing sources, to CERA.

Notes and Sources

Sources of some passages in the text are noted here to acknowledge people who provided anecdotes, to identify the railways which generated the stories or to suggest opportunities for further reading about events that appeared in the newspapers.

You Can Take It with You (chapter 1, pages 4–5)
The quotation on holiday baggage, referring to the Aurora-Yorkville (Ill.) line of the Elgin, Aurora & Southern Traction Company, is from the Aurora *Beacon* of September 6, 1904. The skeleton was found in 1901 on an interurban car of the Union Traction Company of Indiana; it is reported in *Life along the Trolley Line* by David McNeil (published at Cincinnati by the author, 1989). The bank messengers' robbery of 1931 and the list of prohibited articles relate to the Saskatoon (Sask.) Municipal Railway, as quoted in *Saskatoon's Electric Transit* by Easten Wayman (Toronto: Railfare Enterprises, 1988). In Toronto, carrying empty perambulators on the dash while mother and baby rode inside the car was called "putting baby on the hook." In *Street Railways of St. Petersburg Florida* (Forty Fort, Pa.: Harold E. Cox, 1983) Jim Buckley tells of fishermen's catches on the Veteran City line. Norman Carlson recounts the story of his

grandfather Axel Gustafson's carpenter's tool boxes. Thomas A. Carpenter remembers the inevitable coal passers—"nobody minded as long as they stayed on the rear platform!" The cadets were riding North Shore Line cars on The Milwaukee Electric Railway & Light Company on May 30, 1926.

A Hundred and Fifty Pounds Free (chapter 2, pages 6–9)
The "Norfolk Bulletin" issue of *The Headway Recorder* (Washington Division, Electric Railroaders' Assn., 1951) tells about the market service. John J. Walker remembers how bread truck drivers enlisted the help of Des Moines City Railway motormen to take boxes of bread to his father's store at the end of the Urbandale line and to other stores at 49th, 56th and 61st streets. A brief review of the railroad express business is "Decline and Decay of REA" by Robert B. Shaw in July 1979 *Trains* (Milwaukee: Kalmbach).
The collision occurred February 2, 1924, near Fortville on the Union Traction Company of Indiana; the report is that of the Public Service Commission of Indiana.

Their Appointed Rounds (chapter 3, pages 10–13)
A good general reference is *A Short History of the Mail Service* by Carl H. Scheele (Washington: Smithsonian Institution Press, 1970). The streetcar RPO cities were Baltimore, Boston, Brooklyn, Chicago, Cincinnati, Cleveland, New York, Omaha, Philadelphia, Pittsburgh, Rochester, St. Louis, San Francisco, Seattle and Washington. The Indiana mail cars ran until 1941; see *Indiana Railroad, the Magic Interurban* by George K. Bradley (Chicago: Bulletin 128 of the Central Electric Railfans' Assn., 1991). George Krambles recalls mail being picked up "on the fly" at Spokane during his visit in September 1939. *The Story of the B. C. Electric Railway Company* by Henry Ewert (North Vancouver, B. C.: Whitecap Books, 1986) gives good insights into mail carrying by Canada's largest interurban.
"*We* don't consider that safe," scoffed R. E. Jamieson, passenger traffic manager of the Chicago South Shore & South Bend Railroad, at mention of loading papers in the vestibules on other lines. *Spokane's Street Railways: an Illustrated History* (Spokane, Wash.: Inland Empire Railway Historical Society, 1987) tells the effect of newspaper "bombardment" on the flagstop shelters along the Washington Water Power Company interurban lines. Trainmaster Allan C. Williams recalled that in his train service days, the electric suburban trains of the Illinois Central Railroad often had *almost* enough papers to pay the flagman an increment.

From Dairy Farm to City Dairy (chapter 4, pages 14–17)
The water traffic in returning cans was found on the Fraser Valley line of the British Columbia Electric Railway, one of the longer milk runs (76 miles in 4¾ hours). Richard R. Kunz, a North Shore Line relief ticket agent in 1962–1963, found milk tickets at some stations, but no tariff permitting their sale.

Bags, Barrels and Boxes (chapter 5, pages 18–29)
The "over and short" list is from a 1930 circular of the *Central Electric Traffic Association,* a bureau of the interurban roads in Indiana, Ohio and portions of Pennsylvania, Michigan and Kentucky. Problems with security of cigarette loads are mentioned in *Cincinnati & Lake Erie Railroad, Ohio's Great Interurban System* (San Marino, Calif.: Golden West Books, 1974) by Jack Keenan, the son of the road's traffic manager. The accident record covers 1919–1925 at the Gary (Ind.) freight house of the Chicago, Lake Shore & South Bend Railway. The quotation on

platform delivery is from a 1934 freight mileage tariff of the Indiana Railroad, one of the more formal interurbans.

In the Name of Efficiency (chapter 6, pages 30–31)
Articles by Robert E. Mohowski in May 1988 *Railroad Model Craftsman* (Newton, N. J.: Carstens) and by John S. Gallagher Jr. in August 1952 *Trains* (Milwaukee: Kalmbach) put the use of containers and piggyback into perspective.

Pulling the Red Box Cars (chapter 7, pages 32–41)
CA&E traffic statistics are from *Sunset Lines* by Larry Plachno (Polo, Ill.: Transportation Trails, 1989).

Digging Their Own Grave (chapter 8, pages 42–45)
George Gordon provides a vivid description of handling sand and other company materials on the "construction car run" in *Detroit's Street Railways, Volume II* by Jack E. Schramm, William H. Henning and Thomas J. Dworman (Chicago: Bulletin 120 of the Central Electric Railfans' Assn., 1980).

Juice in Its Solid Form (chapter 9, pages 46–49)
Unit trains on the South Shore Line began in 1964 and operated over the Algers, Winslow & Western Railway, Southern Railway and Chicago & Eastern Illinois Railroad. Some papers of the Capitol Car Line may be found at the State Historical Society of North Dakota.
The garbage transfer service at Regina (1913–1946) is well described in *Saskatchewan's Pioneer Streetcars* by Colin K. Hatcher (Montreal: Railfare Enterprises, 1971).

What You See Is What You Get (chapter 10, pages 50–53)
Russ Powell, motorman on the THI&E in 1924–1929, remembers the Purdue drum. John Baxter of Pittsburgh Railways tells the fire-ax story.

Saves Weight and Time (chapter 11, pages 54–55)
Wayne Trambarger of the Union Traction Company of Indiana was interviewed in 1977–1978 by William R. Kearney. Thanks to Elin Christianson of the Hobart (Ind.) Historical Society and Norm Carlson for locating the tape. Trambarger carried the hogs at New Hope, a crossing just south of Sharpsville. J. William Vigrass tells of the potential for traffic to the soup factory via Port Authority Transit Corporation.

Here Comes the Beef (chapter 12, pages 56–57)
The "orange cars" in Rochester are noted in *Canal Boats, Interurbans & Trolleys* by Ron Amberger, Dick Barrett and Greg Marling (Rochester, N. Y.: Rochester Chapter, National Railway Historical Society, 1985). William E. Robertson recalls the North Shore Line refrigerator cars in service, even on the old line before the Skokie Valley Route was opened.

Tanks for Shipping by Trolley (chapter 13, pages 58–59)
American Car & Foundry Company introduced another design of covered hopper in 1961.

Don't Call It a Freight Car (chapter 14, pages 60–65)
John P. Scharle contributed the word imagery of the sound effects when a train negotiated downtown Bethlehem (Pa.). See *The Nickel Plate Story* by John A. Rehor (Milwaukee: Kalmbach, 1965) on the operation to the Northern Ohio Food Terminal.

Many Shapes and Sizes (chapter 15, pages 66–71)
Gas-electric locomotive #100 was built in 1913 by General Electric for the Minneapolis, St. Paul, Rochester & Dubuque, a wannabee electric interurban; went in 1917 to the Central Warehouse Company at St. Paul where it was changed the following year for operation from trolley wire; and in 1922 found its way to the Minneapolis, Anoka & Cuyana Range Railway. The three properties shared an executive. Since 1967 it has been in the

Minnesota Transportation Museum. Builders' catalogs, though not widely available, form a good description of the standard lines of locomotives. *Baldwin Westinghouse Electric Locomotives, 1912* and *Baldwin Westinghouse Electric Locomotives, 1925* (Chicago: Bulletins 23–24 of the Electric Railway Historical Society, 1957) are principally reprints from some of them. The peripatetic locomotive was Auburn & Syracuse #105; Hydro-Electric Power Commission (Ont.) #E-21 (in 1919); Toronto & York Radial Railway #2 (in 1924); Chatham, Wallaceburg & Lake Erie Railway; Niagara, St. Catharines & Toronto Railway #18 (in 1927); and Oshawa Railway #18 (in 1960).

An Obstacle Course (chapter 18, pages 76–79)
Locomotive #196 of the Terre Haute, Indianapolis & Eastern Traction Company featured the lighting of the trolley wire. The Farmers & Mechanics Bank in Ann Arbor (Mich.) was the victim of runaway cars on August 5, 1927; the incident is described in *When Eastern Michigan Rode the Rails III* by Jack E. Schramm, William H. Henning and Richard R. Andrews (Glendale, Calif.: Interurban Press, 1988). North Shore Line conductor John D. Horachek related some of the problems with operating on the gantlets. At Gary (Ind.), the South Shore Line's gantlet was in place until construction of the present low-platform station in 1984. Milwaukee motorman Ed Wilson relates the troubles with a 50-foot box car in *TM* by Joseph M. Canfield (Chicago: Bulletin 112 of the Central Electric Railfans' Assn., 1972). Railroad wheel treads extend $4^{11}/_{32}''$ outside the gauge line, and the flanges are $1''$ deep compared to only $3/_4''$ of typical streetcars.

Pressed into Service (chapter 19, pages 80-83)
In *Traction & Models* (Indianapolis: Vane A. Jones Co.) for September 1967, Carl R. Bogardus, Jr. tells of finishing an Indiana Railroad trip to Scottsburg in a blizzard aboard locomotive #751 because the passenger car's trolley base had been disabled and hence the car could not be heated.

At the Interchange (chapter 20, pages 84–85)
Robert E. Geis tells the story of the Pennsylvania Railroad crew who took a chance to retrieve their cars. The Jamestown, Westfield & Northwestern Railroad interurban car he was riding, not having a coupler at the front end, could be of no help.

What It Takes to Be a Railroad (chapter 21, pages 86–87)
The list of commodities comes from a 1940 tariff of the Pittsburgh Railways Company.

Not Only Electric (chapter 22, pages 88–91)
The Southern New York steam locomotive is displayed today at the Corry (Pa.) Historical Museum in the home town of its builder, the Climax Manufacturing Company. Trolley-pole diesels were found on the Bamberger Railroad in Utah, the Pacific Electric Railway in California and the Portland (Ore.) Traction Company.

Trolley Freight in New York State (chapter 23, pages 92–121)
The greater part of the chapter was prepared by James R. McFarlane. The section on Brooklyn is condensed from an article by Bernard Linder and Karl F. Groh. That on the Metropolitan is condensed from an article written in 1978 for this book by Francis J. Goldsmith, Jr. David Nestle assisted with notes on local pronunciations.

The End of a Hard Day's Work (pages 122–128)
Fred Schneider collected the statistics on freight, express and mail revenue from the United States *Census of Electrical Industries, 1917, 1922, 1927 and 1937.* For the graph the revenues for the first three of those years give a picture of the pattern during the dominant period of the electric railway industry. The conversion to 1992 dollars is based on the urban Consumer Price Index of the U. S. Bureau of Labor Statistics.

Index to Companies and Localities

Also appearing in this index are commodities mentioned in *Not Only Passengers* and glossary entries (railway freight terms defined in the book). The glossary entries are in *italics* in the index as they are in the text.

References are to text on the pages indicated, except that ***italic full face figures*** indicate illustrations or captions. For example, reference is made to the Adams Express Company in the caption to a photo on pages 22–23.

The symbols following index entry **94** are the map coordinates of a city or town appearing on the map on page 94. For example, Albany (N. Y.), **94 M5**, is located on the map where column M and row 5 meet.

Italic full face figures indicate illustrations or captions.
94 F4 indicates map coordinates on page 94.

↑**Niagara Junction Railway locomotives #14, #16 and #9 await crews and assignments on a warm summer evening in 1972.** KEN KRAEMER

↑**Four-truck locomotive #71 raises the dust as it races west through Riverton (Ill.) on March 12, 1955, just before the end of electric operation of the Springfield-Champaign line. Besides some traction equipment—soon to be obsolete—it's hauling several railroad box cars.** GORDON E. LLOYD. **Yes indeed, the Illinois Terminal Railroad carried . . .**